We are in a real crisis here, folks.
growing outward signs and symp
in our police, our national suffering will extend far beyond the tragedy of
police suicide. Tim Rupp offers credible insight and counsel based on raw
first-hand accounts at the crime scene or on the call. Police officers simply
have to realize they are a trinity of body, mind, and spirit. While the work
they do impacts each aspect of this trinity, the spirit is the immortal driver
of them all. Viewing traumatic experiences through a spiritual lens can act
as the impetus of supernatural hope and resilient strength!

If only our police could come to that Truth. The trauma they face will
draw them closer to the virtues they risk their lives for, long for, that protect
for. It will make them better and stronger! This knowledge Tim concisely
writes puts the suffering we see all round us, that permeates our existence,
into proper perspective.

Thank you, Tim for putting this tool in our hands. It is an incredibly
powerful apologetic.

Steve Lambert
Captain (Ret) VA State Police

I have known Tim for over twenty years as a cop, a supervisor, a
pastor, and a friend so I expect insightful biblical perspectives in his books.
Suicide is Not an Option *goes way beyond my expectations. Tim's
passion to serve his brothers and sisters in blue shines throughout, tackling
a difficult topic and a tough group. We are quick to cancel cover officers, bold
to stand up against all odds, and never want to show a vulnerability that
could be mistaken for weakness. We want to separate ourselves from those
that don't understand and make light of the tragedy—as if we are
unscathed. We seek justice in an unjust world, and seldom do we see the
answer to all injustice is to be properly equipped. Every warrior needs to
own and keep a copy so we can equip ourselves properly for the battle.*

Detective Joseph Dubs
San Antonio PD, TX

Everyone associated with law enforcement talks about the problem of officer suicide. By my second year as a police chaplain, I was comforting a detective after a fellow officer took his own life in the police station. Tim Rupp's book Suicide is Not an Option *answers the two questions we always ask: "Why?" and "What could we have done?" Every time I teach a recertification class to area LEOs, I talk about suicide prevention. From now on, I will tell them to read Tim's latest book. We all need hope, and a real reason to live. You will find both in these pages.*

Rev. Chuck Tyree
Pastor and Police Chaplain
Norwich, CT

Suicide is Not an Option *is a must read for anyone involved with law enforcement today! In my 24 years ministering to law enforcement officers, I've had to deal with numerous suicides and officers contemplating suicide. I never really had the right tool or person, who truly understood the pressures of law enforcement to help guide me. I found them.* Suicide is Not an Option *is the right tool and Tim Rupp the right person to help prevent the ever-increasing suicide rate among our brothers and sisters in blue. I highly recommend this book and Tim's book* Winning a Gunfight *as must reads!*

Louisiana State Trooper (Ret.) Larry G. Ledford
President/Founder
No Greater Love Foundation, Inc.

Tim Rupp masterfully explains the spiritual dynamic related to suicide and officer wellness. The wisdom of Proverbs 13:12 says, "Hope deferred makes the heart sick." While discussions on suicide prevention should include aspects of mental and physical health, Tim sheds light on this very important but often missing link. Suicide is Not an Option *is a must read.*

Chaplain and Deputy Jonathan Parker
Hamilton County SO, TN
Pastor, Cop Church Chattanooga

The timing of this book is incredible! Never before has the frustration and fatigue of law enforcement officers been so profuse. I cringe at the idea of law enforcement going away when we know officers are a biblically ordained authority. My hope is that Suicide is Not an Option *will be a means for one more warrior to keep up the faith and stay in the fight, as well as one more family member to sharpen their prayer and efforts alongside their warrior!*

Chaplain Aaron Johnson
St. Bernard SO, LA

Suicide is Not an Option *is very informative, to the point, and very well written.*

Sgt. Jared Hurt
Bonneville County SO, ID
Special Investigations Unit

It was a hopeless and dark time in my life. I wanted the pain to stop and didn't want to go on. Thankfully, I had friends that loved me and helped turn my eyes toward the author of hope. What has followed has been the best years of my life. Suicide is Not an Option *will equip you for that journey. Read it. Soak up the truth within its pages and live!*

Chaplain Jim Bontrager
National Board Member
Fellowship of Christian Peace Officers USA

Tim Rupp has a tremendously unique vantage point as a pastor, military veteran, peace officer, and college professor, on the topic of peace officers and military veterans' suicide. He provides an inspirational and insightful perspective on suicides within these professions. Ultimately, the book is an aid, through the application of hope and faith to the devastating aspect of dealing on a long-term basis with the problems of our society. It can help those in the field of protecting our citizens, to realize that suicide is not an option.

Deputy Chief (Ret.) Joery Smittick
San Antonio PD, TX

One of the things I like best about Tim's books is his perspective. Having been a police officer in San Antonio for many years, He faced and saw many of the things we LEOs have in our careers. Tim's experience as a LEO lends creditability and relevance to those of us still engaged in policing. His involvement in law enforcement coupled with his years of service as a pastor make him uniquely qualified to discuss the subject matter at hand. Whether you are having thoughts of suicide or you have lost hope due to the troubling times we are going through, I highly suggest you read Tim's book which I think will help us regain the Hope that things can and will get better.

Deputy Patrick Crapo
Bonneville County SO, ID

In Suicide is not an Option, *Tim takes us on a journey. The reality of suicide and its impact on those left behind is never in question. It is however, seen more clearly as we read these pages, filled with examples that touch both the heart and the imagination. The issues of hope and faith are key. Relationships with those we know, family, friends, co-workers, and those in our congregations become more important. The Gospel message is presented clearly. Hope in Christ, in relation to our battle with suicide, is discussed in a manner I have never experienced before. As a retired Army Chaplain, during my 25 plus years of active duty and National Guard service, I was asked regularly to provide the annually suicide prevention and awareness training. This training was scripted to Army standards. The spiritual aspect of our being was rarely, if ever, part of the actual curriculum. Finally, a book that speaks to the reality of this truth, "It is Christ in you, the HOPE of glory." Thank you, Tim, for this. Needed today!*

Rev. Bob Collins
Chaplain, U. S. Army (Retired)
Ecclesiastical Endorse for Federal Chaplains
Alliance Chaplain Ministries

SUICIDE IS NOT AN OPTION

OPTION

HOPE IN MAN'S SEARCH FOR MEANING

TIM RUPP

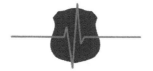

ISBN: 978-1-7325277-2-0

Author Contact Info: office@thestrongblueline.org

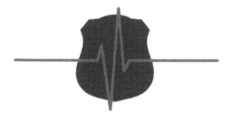

The Strong Blue Line
Idaho Falls, ID
TheStrongBlueLine.org

Cover art by Daniel Sundahl
© 2020 DanSun PhotoArt
DanSunPhotos.com

DEDICATION

To Charlie and Mike, my brothers in blue, who left us too soon. And to the brothers and sisters in blue I worked with, and those who continue to hold the thin blue line.

TABLE OF CONTENTS

ACKNOWLEDGEMENT

Some of the most formative years in a boy's life are his early teenage years. I was thirteen in 1974 when I met the energetic, crazy, fun-loving Stan Ponz and his wife Carol. Stan led the youth group at Florida Bible College, where dad attended classes after he retired from the Air Force. Not only did Stan have a magnetic personality, he had a sincere faith. Young people need to know that truth exists and the adults they look up to live by that unwavering truth. Stan and his wife Carol have exemplified this throughout the five decades I've known them.

Over the years our paths crossed again in San Antonio where Stan pastored, and had a radio and teaching ministry. Finally, while I was pastoring in Idaho, we connected once again, and he invited me to be an associate of Make It Clear Ministries. Stan's charismatic personality and sincere faith endure. Now, on the other end of life, where there are more years behind me than ahead, I continue to lean on him as a friend and mentor.

Stan took the time to read, reread, and read again the initial manuscript. Throughout the project Stan offered counsel and gave suggestions and encouragement. Thank you, Stan for your advice, correction, and encouragement. Stan continues to minister as President of Florida Bible College and Make It Clear Ministries.

Thanks to Jonathan Parker for suggesting and providing questions for group study.

Thanks to Mrs. Cynthia Hazard for encouragement, support, and editing.

Thanks to the many friends who encouraged me to write this book.

Thanks to my wife Sherry for her support, encouragement, and advice.

PREFACE

TIM RUPP, JUNE 2020

In 2019, Attorney General William Barr observed, "There is no tougher job in the country than serving as a law-enforcement officer. Every morning, officers across the country get up, kiss their loved ones and put on their protective vests. They head out on patrol never knowing what threats and trials they will face. And their families endure restless nights, so we can sleep peacefully."[1] Shockingly, there is a greater chance of a law enforcement officer (LEO) dying by suicide than by being murdered.

This book is written to LEOs and military combat veterans, their families, their friends, and those who want to help. For most of these warriors the world is black and white. It is full of good guys and bad guys. The warriors are those Lt. Col. Dave Grossman has dubbed "sheepdogs." The bad guys (and gals) are the wolves, the criminals, the terrorists—evil people who will not hesitate to steal, kill, or destroy to get what they want. At stake are the innocents. The innocents are the sheep, blindly wandering through life oblivious to the danger that surrounds them.

Warriors have a mission. They protect the innocents and stop the bad guys. It's that simple. But warriors are not machines; they are human beings who possess a body, soul, and spirit. Ever since the beginning of warfare and policing, soldiers and LEOs have been trained in tactics. In fact, tactical training eats up a large chunk of the military's and an agency's time and budget. In the 1990s, Lt. Col. Grossman shed light on the impor-

tance of training and preparing the mind. In 2016, I wrote Winning a Gunfight *and emphasized the importance of training the whole person how to win a gunfight body, soul, and spirit. Like ignoring the mind, it is unwise to ignore the spirit. Why do we ignore one third of who we are? To be politically correct? So, we don't offend a few sensitive people by mentioning religion or God? Some insist on separating God from government, but it's futile to attempt separating God from the warrior.*

Warriors don't care. They want the best training and preparation they can get to accomplish their mission. They want it straight. They're looking for facts. They're not afraid to train their whole self—they want to. If they don't agree, be it tactical, mental, or spiritual, they can process the information and take what makes sense to them. I write direct and to the point, the way warriors want it. They can determine what they'll take and what they'll leave.

Writing about suicide is scary, but the issue must be addressed. My hope is that this book will reduce suicides among law enforcement officers and combat veterans, or anyone for that matter. How does one do that? Mental health professionals have been available to police officers for years, yet from the limited data available, the suicide rate among officers continues to rise. The fact is, most mental health professionals will readily admit they have little or no training in spiritual matters. So, let's address the spiritual head-on.

I've been a police officer and/or a pastor my whole life. That's all I've ever been. Now I'm a law enforcement chaplain. I understand the law enforcement subculture and how to communicate to LEOs. I tell stories to which warriors can relate and will help give perspective to those not familiar with policing. Some stories might be offensive—sorry.

In preparing to write, one of the resources I read was Man's Search for Meaning *by Viktor Frankl. He survived WWII Nazi concentration camps and was a neurologist and psychiatrist. In* Man's Search for Meaning, *Frankl spoke of three woes common to all people which he called the triad of tragedy: pain, guilt, and death. Are there answers to these three woes that beset us? Is there hope for something better? Will pain ever end, will guilt ever be relieved, will death ever be conquered?*

SUICIDE IS NOT AN OPTION

"So now faith, hope, and love abide,
these three; but the greatest of these is love."
(1 Corinthians 13:13)

Life is simple.
Death is simple.
It's living that complicates things.

1

PARADISE LOST

Warriors, the flower of Heaven, once yours, now lost.
—John Milton

Charles Thompson walked up to the blackboard in front of San Antonio Police Department (SAPD) Cadet Class 83-B. He stopped, grabbed a piece of chalk, and drew a large circle. Above the circle he wrote "Sergeant-at-Arms." He put the chalk down, turned around to face the class and with a huge smile, stepped in front of the circle. The class broke out into laughter. Charlie had my vote.

"Tall, dark, and handsome" is how I suppose most ladies described Charlie. But he was more than good looks. He had a contagious laugh and a permanent smile to go with his short Afro and silver wire-rim glasses. At age twenty-one he was one of the youngest cadets in our class.

Charlie and I became friends during the five-month cadet class that started on July 11, 1983 and concluded a couple weeks before Christmas. Then again, Charlie was friends with everyone. He was voted into office unanimously. Charlie loved calling the meetings to order and dismissing them with a loud and unnecessary "Attention!" and "Dismissed!"

The 33 of us who made it to graduation, drew patrol assignments all over the city. I was assigned to the 3-11 (3:00 p.m. to 11:00 p.m.) downtown "one-section." Charlie drew the same shift, but was assigned to the northeast beat, the "seven-section." At the time, the SAPD had only one substation on the city's far westside. So, I saw Charlie daily, along with the hundred plus other officers at roll call. But working different areas of the city meant we rarely saw each other after the daily briefing.

Our cadet class got a quick taste of policing—*baptism by fire*, they say. On Christmas Eve of 1983, veteran Officer Gilbert Ramirez was gunned down by a man with a shotgun on the city's Southside. Within a month of graduation, I attended my first police funeral. The mortician did a good job repairing the gunshot wound to Gilbert's face and nearly forty years later I can still clearly see the uniformed body lying in the casket as hundreds of officers filed by. Shortly after Gilbert was murdered, two of our classmates quit the department. I don't know if it had anything to do with the reality of police work. Most often, new police officers are called "rookies;" on the SAPD, a rookie officer is called a "boot." At the time, we all wore black Red Wing® boots, and a rookie was a "new-boot" or simply a "boot." I couldn't wait until my boots showed some signs of wear. As a young boot, I quickly learned why officers retreat into their own subculture.

The San Antonio River meanders slowly through the heart of the city. Both sides of the river are reinforced with concrete walls to keep the river safely in its banks and to provide a picturesque Riverwalk. In summer, the river is low and about four feet below the top of the wall. Before major restoration of the downtown area that began in the 1990s, the river south of downtown was a gathering place for drunks to hang out. Pardon me, perhaps I should refer to these gentlemen as "intoxicated persons" or "homeless" but that was before political correctness, and officers tend to call things as they see it. Don't mistake the label as disrespectful or insensitive, it simply reflects reality. Law enforcement officers (LEOs) are into reality—what is real. Every day they deal with the realities of life—and death. As a result, they build in defense mechanisms to preserve their own souls. One mechanism is seeing people as responsible for their own actions. Imagine that, people responsible for their own choices.

In the summer of 1984, I received a call for a man in the river, just south of downtown. To seek relief from the summer's scorching heat, children often played in the river. It was also common for a drunk to end up in the river, either intentionally or otherwise, and not be able to climb out. I arrived in the area, parked my cruiser, and walked over to the riverbank. Fifty yards to the south was a fifty-something Hispanic male flopping around in the river, screaming, "I'm drowning! I'm drowning!" I walked along the bank and yelled out to the man, "Stand up!" He stopped and looked at me. I repeated, "Stand up!" He stood in the two and half-feet deep water and walked over to me. I pulled him from the river, sat him down, and called the wagon to transport him to the detoxification holding tank. In the mid-80's SAPD had three cargo vans that were used as "paddy-wagons" to transport drunks or violent prisoners. When the regular wagon-driver was off, boot officers were assigned to drive the wagon. Charlie had wagon duty that day.

He showed up, with his characteristic smile, took the prisoner off my hands, and loaded him up in the back of the wagon. We laughed about the call and chatted for a while catching up on our classmates and what was going on in our lives. "Are you going to marry that gal you were dating in the academy?" I asked. Charlie just smiled, "I don't know, Tim."

I finished the booking slip and gave it to Charlie, "Here, you go, I'll talk to you later."

"Okay, see ya later," Charlie said and with a wave good-bye he was gone.

I never saw Charlie again. Days later, on August 9, 1984, Charlie took his own life.

Not only were the members of cadet class 83-B shocked, so too was anyone who knew Charlie. Some officers refused to believe the homicide detectives and started to spread the rumor that Charlie's death was an accident. They claimed Charlie accidentally shot himself while cleaning his service revolver. Charlie died from a single gunshot wound to the head. We carried Smith and Wesson, model 65, .357 magnum revolvers. They are safe guns. Charlie was well trained; he knew how to handle the weapon. No, it wasn't an accident. As much as we'd like to think it was, it wasn't. The reality is Charlie died by suicide.

Why? Why, of all people Charlie? It didn't make any sense. Gilbert was gunned down, murdered by a man with a shotgun. Tragic and shocking, but it made sense. A bad guy was responsible. Downtown drunks falling into the river was also logical. If you drink too much bad things happen. That makes sense. But Charlie? Why did a young man with a promising career end his own life? That doesn't make sense.

But not only Charlie, why do LEOs take their own lives at a disproportionately high rate compared to the general population?[1] Is it because of what they see and do on the job? Becoming a police officer was a huge wakeup call for me. I learned more about humanity than I cared to know.

~

That year was a tough year for us. In 1984, four SAPD officers took their own lives. I didn't get it; and like many of my fellow officers, I asked why. Oh, we really didn't ask anyone for an answer, we just kept the question inside and went about our work. For years the question remained unanswered. It wasn't something I thought about all the time, but it was part of the job. Suicide is something LEOs think about more than most people because they regularly respond to calls for suicides and attempted suicides. The "why" question always lingers.

Not that there weren't plenty of people willing to give answers. At the annual in-service training classes, we learned that psychiatrists, psychologists, and a number of other mental health professionals blame suicide on depression, schizophrenia, anxiety, panic, substance abuse, and a number of other "mental illnesses" that result in ending one's own life. Research seems to back up those assumptions. An article on the National Center for Biotechnology Information's website reported that over 90 percent of suicides in the United States are associated with mental illness that includes alcohol and/or substance abuse.[2] So have the mental health professionals helped lower the suicide rate? No; they haven't. In fact, over a sixteen-year period (2001 to 2017) the total suicide rate increased 31 percent from 10.7 to 14.0 per 100,000.[3]

Does that mean mental health professionals haven't prevented any suicides? No. Mental health professionals do a good job treating mental illnesses; just like physical health professionals do a good job treating physical illnesses. The data simply reveal the fact that the suicide rate in the United States is on the rise and has been for several years. But what if the problem isn't a mental health issue? When officers get shot, they are rushed to a hospital with a trauma center where doctors and nurses treat them. Physical wounds are treated by physical health professionals. Every effort is made to stop any bleeding, ensure the heart is beating, and the patient is breathing. The body is treated. The physical body was harmed, and the physical body is treated. It would be foolish to rush an officer who was just shot to a psychologist for a counseling session. Mental health care professionals are trained to deal with mental health, not physical. But there's more to a human being than just the physical and mental; there's also a spiritual side.

No one can honestly deny that humans have a spiritual capacity. What that means is interpreted differently. But the fact remains, in addition to the physical and mental, there's a spiritual aspect to each one of us. Humans possess something animals do not—a *spiritual* or a *God*-awareness.

As an atheist, Sigmund Freud denied human spirituality and tried to explain everything through psychoanalysis. He believed religion to be an expression of an underlying mental illness. Surprisingly, although the vast majority of Americans are not atheists, many still hold to Freud's theories and look to psychoanalysis for counsel in spiritual matters.

An understudy of Freud, the noted Austrian neurologist and psychiatrist Viktor Frankl, disagreed with Freud. Frankl who earned both an M.D. and Ph.D. was also a Holocaust survivor and author of

Man's Search for Meaning. The book details Frankl's experiences and those of his fellow prisoners in Nazi concentration camps. Frankl was Jewish and his second wife (his first wife died in a concentration camp) was Roman Catholic. As both a medical doctor and psychiatrist he understood that there is a difference between the mental and spiritual. He wrote about the difficulty of Nazi prisoners adjusting to life after being released, "the man who has suddenly been liberated from mental pressure can suffer damage to his moral and spiritual health."[4] Although linked, the spiritual is distinct from the mental.

Christian theologians call the three parts of humans the *tripartite* view of humanity. Two Bible verses commonly used to support the *tripartite* view are: "And the very God of peace sanctify you wholly; and I pray God your whole *spirit* and *soul* and *body* be preserved blameless unto the coming of our Lord Jesus Christ"[5] and "For the word of God is living and active, sharper than any two-edged sword, piercing to the division of *soul* and of *spirit*, of joints and marrow, and discerning the thoughts and intentions of the heart."[6] Another position, which holds that the soul and spirit are used interchangeably, is the *bipartite* view—that humans have but two parts. This view may be seen as the body and soul/spirit. No matter the view a person holds to, the fact remains humans are physical, mental, and spiritual beings.

Humanity's God-awareness or spirituality causes us to do things animals do not. In *Winning a Gunfight* I wrote:

Animals don't worship. Animals react and respond instinctively. They protect themselves and their own without regard to law or rules of engagement. Animals kill other animals without regard to ethical implications. And they don't know right from wrong. Mankind is different. We worship, react and respond out of reason— or even against reason! We protect our own, but do so with regard to law and rules of engagement. We act with regard to *ethical* implications. We know right from wrong.[7]

It is critical to distinguish the differences between the mental and the spiritual. Although both are part of the whole person, the mental and spiritual are as different as a person's eyes and ears. Eyes and ears are both part of the body, but are significantly different; and as such, they need to be treated differently. The same is true for a person's soul and spirit. To help make the distinction, it might be helpful to think of them as a person's mind and heart. Don't think of the physical brain or heart, but what we think of when we use these terms. We think of reasoning with our mind, but our heart gives us a sense of right and wrong, compassion, spiritual awareness, and the like. When a person acts outside of what is considered normal, we attempt to understand their actions. Take for example the person who commits mass murder. On one hand we try to process the criminal's actions rationally. We try to make sense of it. But when it doesn't make sense, we say things like, "He's lost his mind" or "She's out of her mind." But when that doesn't do, we say their actions are evil. But where does our sense of evil come from? Did our sense of morality evolve through natural selection?

Outside of a supreme and moral being that humanity must answer to, a sense of morality flies in the face of natural selection and survival of the fittest. Why do we allow the physically and mentally disabled to live? How can they contribute to the physical survival of humanity? If in the end, nothing matters but survival, why do we care about the least of us? We care because we are moral creatures. The Judeo-Christian understanding is that humanity was created in the image of God and every human being has intrinsic value to the Creator. Hence, everyone has value. Why? Because survival of the species is not the end game. There's more to life than our earthly existence.

Morality also flies in the face of atheists. Who determines what is moral? The majority of people? The person or people in power? The strongest, richest, or smartest? Are we willing to trust another human being to decide what is moral or immoral? While we like to bicker over little things, everyone has a basic sense of right and wrong. One of the first sentences a child puts together is, "That's not fair!" Intrinsically we know murder, rape, assault, and theft are wrong. Of course, murder is wrong. It depletes the human species and left unchecked it may bring humanity to an end and that would go against basic evolutionary principles. But what about rape? One could argue that a man forcing himself on a woman can actually lead to a larger population of the species. I don't think that will fly in court.

But make no mistake, although the body, soul, and spirit are separate they are all part of the whole person and when one is harmed the others are affected. This is easily seen in life-threatening or significant life-changing events.

In *Winning a Gunfight* my goal is to help train LEOs, combat veterans, and others who arm themselves to win a gunfight tactically, mentally, and ethically—or body, soul, and spirit. All three, body, soul, and spirit, must be properly trained and prepared.

We train the body to tactically win a gunfight by learning to use cover, concealment, and movement. We also learn foundational and combat shooting skills. Ballistic vests are issued to help protect vital organs. If we are hit, we seek medical help to treat and heal the wound. But the physical isn't all we train to protect. We also train the mind to mentally win a gunfight through decision making, shoot-don't shoot scenario training, and reality-based-training. Further, we train LEOs and soldiers that in a gunfight they will likely experience sensory distortions—things such as tunnel vision, diminished sounds, memory loss, intrusive thoughts, time distortions, etc. But we've neglected to train the spirit to win a gunfight. In *Winning a Gunfight*, I made the case that the spiritual is our ethical part; it gives us a sense of right and wrong. We are different from animals. Animals kill without regard to ethics, penal law, or rules of engagement. Humans are different.

We wouldn't go to a mental health specialist to treat a broken leg, so why go to one to treat a spiritual matter? As stated, the body, soul, and spirit are all part of the whole and each affects the other. However, just as mental health professionals specialize in mental health, clergies specialize in spiritual health. The neurologist and psychiatrist Viktor Frankl wrote,

> Some of the people who nowadays call on a psychiatrist would have
> seen a pastor, priest or rabbi in former days. Now they often refuse

to be handed over to a clergyman and instead confront the doctor with questions such as, "What is the meaning of my life?"[8]

Physical health care professionals have a base from which to start. They know what is "normal" for most people. When things are out of whack, they make a treatment plan to bring the body back to normal. Mental health care professionals do the same. There's acceptable behavior or cognitive processes that are considered "normal" for most people. When things are out of whack, they make a treatment plan to bring the soul back to normal. What about the spiritual? What is normal? What is common to most people?

As mentioned, survival of the species is not the end game. There's more to life than a physical body and the ability to reason. There's more to life than our earthly existence. There's more to life than today. There's tomorrow. There is a light that burns inside the heart of humanity—that light is called hope.

2

THE LIGHT OF HOPE

If the light of hope goes out, life shrinks to mere existence, something far less than life was meant to be.
—J.I. Packer.[1]

Hope is intrinsic to humanity. Inside every individual is a sense of hope. Hope for more, hope for something better, hope for the future. What causes the light of hope in law enforcement officers and combat veterans to go out? Is it something related to their culture?

The police subculture is different from any other. Many professions, careers, or occupations have specific subcultures. But policing is uniquely different. Far too often law enforcement officers (LEOs) become cynical and distrust anyone outside of the law enforcement subculture. This is both taught and learned. It's taught in the training academy to cadets, in the police cruiser to rookie officers, and reinforced by media, local governments, and police hate groups. To this day, I recall one of the training officers in the police academy telling our class, "FTP doesn't stand for Free the People!" Disrespect for authority was new to me. My Air Force father taught my brothers and me to respect authority. Maybe that's one reason my brother Ron and I chose policing as a career. I'd like to give you a glimpse into that unique subculture.

Like most American LEOs, I came from a typical middle-class family. My dad was in the Air Force and my mom was a stay-at-home mother to three boys. I am the middle son. Ron is less than two years older and Steve four years younger. Steve has Down syndrome and lived in a private care facility my last few years at home. Dad retired from the service in 1973, went to Bible College, and in 1977 planted a church in Converse, TX, a suburb of San Antonio. Ron graduated from high school in 1978 and enlisted in the Air Force as a Security Police Officer. The following year, I did the same. After his enlistment, Ron joined the SAPD. A year later, I followed suit.

As an eighteen-year-old Air Force Security Police Officer, in a small way, I saw how humanity treated each other. That was new to me. But four years later, policing in San Antonio really opened the eyes of a young, naive twenty-two-year-old. I got a glimpse of reality on my first night out as a police cadet. To become familiar with policing, SAPD procedures, and to get some hands-on training, cadets were required to ride along with a Field Training Officer (FTO) for ten weekend shifts during the police academy. The first ride-along was about five weeks into the 22-week academy. I drew the "dogwatch" shift. Dogwatch is the 11 p.m. to 7 a.m. shift. It was named dogwatch because after about 3 a.m., the only thing that remained on the streets were dogs, criminals, and cops.

Downtown roll call was held in the basement of the SAPD headquarters building at 214 W. Nueva Street. I found a parking spot a couple blocks away, parked my truck, ensured I had a pen and notepad in my pocket, and headed for the building. Several officers were also parking their personal cars and walking toward headquarters. No one made eye contact or acknowledged me. I understood, it was part of the police culture. Being accepted had to be earned, it wasn't given. There was too much at stake.

Roll call was held in a large room with some 300 theater chairs that faced an elevated stage. Seventy or so officers filled the back few rows or stood along either side talking, laughing, cutting up, and ignoring the four cadets seated in the front row. I walked into the intimidating scene and took a seat next to my classmates. Cadets stood out like sore thumbs. We looked like custodians in our blue uniforms, black leather belts, and new black boots. A black open-faced pouch on our belt carried a pair of stainless-steel handcuffs. On each shirt sleeve was a small gold and blue moon-shaped patch that read "Cadet." A shiny silver tag bearing our last name was pinned over the right breast pocket. A royal blue ball cap that bore the image of the SAPD shoulder patch, Alamo and all, sat smartly on our heads. We sat next to each other in silence and waited.

At precisely 10:45 p.m. the shift lieutenant emerged from the patrol office, clipboard in hand, and climbed the stairs onto the stage. He walked to the side of the lectern, leaned on it with his left elbow, and paused. He looked over the top of his reading glasses at the officers in the back of the room, most in an "I don't care" slouch. His gaze then went to the five cadets seated side by side, upright, with their feet on the floor. Self-conscious, we all stared back with notepad and pen in hand ready to scribble down instructions. He looked at each of us as if sizing us up. He wasn't impressed. He looked back to the officers, "Listen up!" The room became quiet—mostly. The lieutenant monotonously read the latest general order from the chief and reminded officers to read the daily bulletin. During this time, most officers listened, but there was still a spattering of small talk among some of the officers. The lieutenant flipped the page on the clipboard and announced, "Roll call!" The room fell silent.

"Borg!" he said in a loud voice.

"Here sir," the officer responded.

"One-one."

"White."

"Sir."

"One-two."

"Rios."

"Here, sir."

"One-three."

And so it went. Then he got to district one-six, "Alvarez[2]."

"Sir."

"One-six."

"Rupp."

As ordered by the academy instructors, I stood (unlike the officers), and said, "Here, sir."

The jeers, taunts, and paper balls came from the back of the room, "Boo, boo!" "Sit down!" they shouted and threw wadded up daily bulletins at me.

"You're with Alvarez," the lieutenant said.

"Yes, sir," I replied and looked behind me to find Officer Alvarez. Nobody offered any help. I sat back down.

The next cadet called on was short and when he stood up, someone in the back yelled, "Stand up!"

Another officer quipped, "He is!"

The room erupted in laughter.

It was part of the culture. The testing began. Each test must be passed. If you can't take a joke, look for another line of work.

After roll call, everyone immediately headed out the doors, into the hallway, and up the stairs that led to the main floor. Half the officers went to the parking lot to find their cars; the other half went to the gas pumps and waited for the previous shift to return the cars. I looked around and tried to find Officer Alvarez. He didn't bother to find me and introduce himself, or even wait for me. I went outside with everyone else and tried to read name tags. No one seemed to be concerned about my dilemma. In fact, most seemed to enjoy it. At the gas pumps I found an officer I knew and asked for help. He pointed out an older Hispanic officer standing by himself waiting at the gas pumps for his car. The officer was a serious looking man with an impeccable uniform. His police hat was tucked under his left arm and a swivel clamshell holster swung gently at his right side. Streaks of gray highlighted jet-black hair that was combed straight back. His boots were shined to a high gloss.

I introduced myself. He looked at me and nodded. He didn't strike me as much of a talker; neither was I. It was going to be a long night. Law enforcement officers come in all shapes and sizes. Some are loud and outgoing. Some are quiet and reserved. They come from all walks of life, from every ethnic group, background, and social class.

But unlike most people, officers are kept at arm's length. Much of this is their own doing. They are hard to understand. Some say they are arrogant, egotistical, pigheaded, or overconfident. Some are. Perhaps it comes from their warrior heart. God gives each of us a heart and a personality to do what he has called us to do. No matter the personality he gives, we can take it to the extreme. Warriors are no different.

Warriors do the things others don't have the heart to do. I've heard many people say, "I could never be a police officer." Why? It's because what officers are called to do. Where they are called to go, what they are called to see, and how they are expected to show restraint.

Warriors do things most people consider foolish. Danger is almost like a drug that keeps warriors going, and that is troubling. In fact, that scares some. Not everyone likes the police. Some resent them. Some even disdain them. Some don't like LEOs because they are authority figures. Some don't like them because they don't understand them. Some don't like them because they are envious of their bravery. Some don't like them because they've been hurt by them. The hurt may have been physical, financial, or emotional. Sadly, sometimes these hurts are real and unwarranted.

The 3-11 officer was on a late call and I stood awkwardly silent next to Officer Alvarez waiting for our car to be returned. Finally, it arrived. We gassed it up and Alvarez checked in service, "10-8, 1-6."

The dispatcher responded, "10-4, 1-6."

As were many officers at the time, Alvarez was Vietnam veteran. After he learned I was a post-Vietnam Air Force veteran, he lightened up a bit. But still he didn't talk much as we cruised slowly around San Antonio's dark streets. It was unusually slow for a Saturday night. He answered my questions and was a willing teacher. I just had to ask, listen, and watch. Our first call was for a disturbance. Our complainant was an Hispanic female. The whole exchange between her and Alvarez was carried out in Spanish, and I didn't have a clue what happened. Alvarez explained after we finished and were back in service. He gave me the information I needed for my report.

The emergency tone sounded a couple times, but to my disappointment, the calls were for other areas in the city. Shortly after one

a.m., we received a call to the 100 block of Kearney Street for a disturbance, a man with a gun. We arrived and discovered there had been a
shooting with one person hit. Emergency Medical Service (EMS) was
called and transported the victim to the hospital. The suspect fled
before we arrived. The shooting happened across the street from the
residence in an open field. We secured the scene, waited for detectives to arrive, and searched for evidence. We found a small caliber
pistol and I was assigned to standby with the gun until a uniformed
detective processed the scene and collected the evidence.

The whole time, from the initial call until we were back in service,
Officer Alvarez never showed excitement or alarm. He just went
about his business like any other call. A couple hours later we were
notified that the victim died. The suspect was arrested at another
location and booked for murder. What struck me about the call was
the fact that the officers went about their job like it was business as
usual. A human being was just murdered by another, and it was
simply par for the course. Life goes on. Welcome to police work.

The law enforcement subculture isn't only taught, it is learned.
It's learned on the streets when officers realize what the "thin
blue line" means. One thing it means is that officers are on their own
—they don't look for help when being assaulted. Assaults on officers
occur far more often than people realize. According to the FBI, in
2018 law enforcement agencies reported nearly sixty thousand
assaults on officers. This made the rate of assault 10.8 per 100 sworn
officers for the year.[3] However, the data collected only reflects the
reported physical assaults on officers. This doesn't include the scuf-
fles, resisting arrests, and many other physical confrontations that
don't make the FBI's Uniform Crime Report statistics.

During my career I was assaulted (verbally and physically), had to
forcibly take down prisoners who resisted arrest, and break-up a
number of fights. Not once did a citizen step in and help. There were
those who watched, some even called for help, but no one ever
stepped in to help. I don't believe it's because people didn't care. I

believe it's because most were fearful, didn't know how to help, or assumed I could take care of myself and didn't need or want their assistance. The inaction of citizens makes it easy for young officers to get caught up in the "us versus them" game. "Them" being anyone not wearing a badge. Because of their inaction, many officers assume citizens don't care. Some don't, but most do; they just don't know how to help. Nonetheless, this creates cynicism and reinforces the belief that no one can be trusted unless they're wearing a badge.

Every day, officers across America are involved in shootings. In *Winning is More than Surviving,* I remind clergy,

> Nearly everyone who holds a job is at times preoccupied with thoughts of making a bad decision. Police officers are no exception. While some professions (i.e., surgeons and emergency medical professionals) require life and death decisions, there's nothing quite like the life and death decisions police officers (and combat soldiers) make daily in a variety of situations. The decisions medical personnel make aim to save life. Police officers and military combatants make decisions to take life. While the result may be the same— the death of a human being—there's a difference.
>
> It's common for officers to be haunted by dreams and thoughts about whether they will respond properly at the moment of truth. Will the decision be *morally* correct? Will the decision be *legally* correct? Will the decision be *administratively* correct?
>
> Even when officers and soldiers are justified using deadly force, killing another human being can be traumatizing. Consequently, it's important for them to be at peace spiritually with the possibility of taking the life of another human being.[4]

Although most officers will complete their career without being involved in a shooting, it's always on their mind. Policing is a dangerous occupation. Not only is there the threat of being assaulted or shot, there's the danger of driving at high speeds, being infected by disease, and numerous other risks officers take that bind them together. During my twenty-four-year career on the SAPD, seventeen officers were killed in the line of duty. This doesn't account for the officers who died while off duty by natural causes, accident, or suicide. Funerals have a way of binding people together.

Then there's the everyday grind. Law enforcement officers never know what their next call will be, and that's some of the attraction to the profession. On a typical eight-hour shift in San Antonio, an officer may handle an automobile accident, three or four domestic disturbances (if not more), a couple other disturbances or fights, an intoxicated person, a shoplifter, make an arrest or two, and take a burglary report. Sprinkled in over the course of a typical month will be a high-speed vehicular pursuit, a shooting, suicide, and/or a natural death. Sometimes they come in waves. I remember a summer night on San Antonio's Eastside, we had four shootings with people shot at each separate location.

Then there are the calls for injured officers. When officers are harmed by accident (whether on or off-duty) who handles the call? Fellow officers. Law enforcement officers are called to pick up the pieces, investigate, and if necessary, file charges. Working the variety of calls, seeing what they see, and doing what they do helps to form the unique bond among LEOs. Officers trust each other with their lives, they experience tragedy together, and laugh it off together, or keep quiet about it together.

The police culture gives context, but it doesn't answer *why*. Why do some officers opt for suicide?

L aw enforcement agencies across the country, be they federal, state, local, or tribal, spend millions of dollars keeping LEOs alive. They provide initial training, recurring training, firearms, and protective gear to help keep officers safe. And most of the time officers are kept alive. Below 100, a non-profit organization, is on a mission to reduce line-of-duty-deaths among our nation's LEOs to below 100 annually, which hasn't been seen since 1943. Their noble vision is to "eliminate preventable line-of-duty police deaths and serious injuries through compelling common-sense training designed to focus on areas under an officer's control."[5] Below 100 champions five principles to attain the thus far elusive goal: 1. Wear your seatbelt; 2. Watch your speed; 3. Wear your vest; 4. W.I.N. (pay attention to "What's Important Now?"); and 5. Remember: Complacency kills. These five principles are directed at driving, tactics, and situational awareness.

Training, equipment, awareness, and great medical care all contribute to a lower (yet not below 100) annual line-of-duty fatality rate for LEOs. According to the Officer Down Memorial Page (odmr.org), from the years 2016 to 2019, a total of 696 LEOs died in the line-of-duty. This is an average of 174 per year. Sadly, there's a more shocking statistic than the number of line-of-duty deaths—suicides. In January 2016, Blue HELP (Honor, Educate, Lead, Prevent) began collecting data on officer suicides. From the years 2016 to 2019 there have been 717 reported suicides of LEOs.[6] This is an average of 179 per year. However, for a number of reasons, it is likely that the actual number of suicides is higher—maybe much higher.

Law enforcement agencies don't routinely keep statistics on officer suicides. It's not that the cause of death isn't accurately reported, it's that suicides aren't categorized as LEOs or non-LEOs. Unless an officer dies by suicide on-duty, the case will simply be recorded as would any other suicide. When researching for this book, I contacted an old friend who still works at the SAPD Homicide Office. He told me what I suspected, the SAPD doesn't track or keep data on officer suicides. Data collected by Blue HELP comes from their own research and volunteer reporting on Blue HELP's website. No doubt, there are some (maybe *many*) that are missed. Further, suicide isn't always the apparent cause of death. Some deaths that are reported as accidental are actually suicide. This is especially true for single-vehicle accidents.

What do the statistics tell us? They tell us LEOs are more likely to die by suicide than in the line of duty; and three times more likely to die by suicide than by being murdered on duty.

The statistical data gives cause for alarm, but it doesn't answer *why*. Why do some officers opt for suicide?

~

Chris Jaramillo, a combat veteran whose police officer father died of suicide in 1992, divulged in a Fox News interview how he turned to drinking to solve his problem. Here's what he said,

> Veterans experience similar traumas to police officers, witnessing scenes that aren't pleasant. As a veteran, I didn't want to ask for help because it wasn't the thing to do, because you got the stigma of being labeled with a mental illness and just like police officers, it wasn't something you bring up.... You drink, you go hang out with your buddies and that is how you deal with it.[7]

Law enforcement officers also opt for other unhealthy behavior such as drug abuse and unnecessary risk-taking activities. They may even turn a healthy activity, such as exercise, into an unhealthy obsession. These activities often lead to relationship problems at home and on the job. Even so, officers find themselves caught up in addictions, substance abuse, needless dangerous or unhealthy activities, and domestic problems. Many people point to these as the *why*. But are these—like suicide—simply options that mask the real issue? Are these symptoms of a deeper problem?

Unhealthy behavior needs to be addressed, but it doesn't answer *why*. Why do some officers opt for suicide?

Then what's the answer? Why is suicide seen as an option? Here's why: the light of hope has gone out.

3

HOPE IS WHY WE LIVE

While there's life, there's hope.
—Marcus Tullius Cicero

On August 20th, 2015, 47-year-old San Antonio Police Captain Mike Gorham drove into the parking lot of Grace Bible Church in La Vernia, TX and ended his life. He was married to Darlene his high school sweetheart of 23 years with whom he shared two children. The obituary described Mike as "a loving husband and father with an incredible sense of humor, a warm smile and a contagious laugh" and "a strong Christian man, [whose] faith was evident to his family and friends."

Mike was a friend and I can testify to his profession as a Christian, sense of humor, and upbeat personality. He was physically healthy and nearing the end of a successful career at the time of his death. As with Charlie, we were shocked. Shortly after Mike's death I talked to a good friend to both Mike and me. He said he spoke to Mike a just a couple hours before the suicide and he showed no signs of being upset or out-of-sorts. Why then did he die by suicide?

Mike was also a man driven to succeed and wanted to be

promoted to deputy chief. However, he was put in a position to choose between being honest about an investigation he was involved in and protecting another high-ranking officer. He desperately wanted to do the right thing and tell the truth. That choice might have ended his career, and certainly may end any hope of being promoted. The details of the investigation are not important. What is important is that Mike wasn't thinking clearly. In his Christian faith, he knew some things to be true, yet he didn't act on what he knew was true, but on what he feared might happen.

What did Mike know was true about his Christian faith? He knew what the Apostle Paul meant when he wrote, "So now faith, hope, and love abide, these three; but the greatest of these is love."[1] Mike had faith in Christ for his salvation. He had the hope of eternal life because his sins were forgiven on the cross and he received God's free gift of salvation. I believe Mike understood God's complete forgiveness. Even forgiving his suicide. That's why he went to the church where he felt safe. After Mike's suicide a friend of his told me in an interview that Mike's family found passages highlighted in his personal Bible about God's forgiveness. Why then did Mike take his own life? Because he lost hope. Not hope in his eternal salvation but hope in humanity. He might have felt that the shame was too much to bear and that his family would be better off without him. He was wrong. No doubt, things would have been different. Perhaps much different, but better with Mike than without him.

~

Charlie Thompson and Mike Gorham opted for suicide because they lost hope. *They lost hope.* Is it really that simple? Yes, it is. The Bible records seven men who died by suicide. Let's look at why they opted for suicide.

The Old Testament records six suicides. Two of these were men who received mortal wounds and knew they were going to die. The first was Abimelech, a son of Gideon, who attempted to become king during the time of the Judges. In battle, a woman threw a millstone from a tower and crushed his head. Knowing he was mortally wounded, he called out to his armor-bearer and said, "Draw your sword and kill me, lest they say of me, 'A woman killed him.'"[2] After receiving a mortal wound Abimelech ordered his own death to save his pride.

King Saul, Israel's first king, was also mortally wounded in battle and fearing the enemy would capture and torture him, ordered his armor-bearer to kill him. The armor-bearer refused, and Saul took his own life to avoid being abused and murdered. Here's the account: Saul commanded, "'Draw your sword, and thrust me through with it, lest these uncircumcised come and thrust me through, and mistreat me.' But his armor-bearer would not, for he feared greatly. Therefore Saul took his own sword and fell upon it."[3] After receiving a mortal wound and in an effort to avoid further pain, Saul killed himself.

Although not mortally wounded, Samson killed himself while taking out thousands of Israel's enemies. After Delilah betrayed him, Samson was blinded and imprisoned by the Philistines. During a festival, he was brought from the prison to entertain his captors. He stood between the pillars that held up the coliseum. The Bible records what happened next:

> Then Samson called to the Lord and said, "O Lord God, please remember me and please strengthen me only this once, O God, that I may be avenged on the Philistines for my two eyes." And Samson grasped the two middle pillars on which the house rested, and he leaned his weight against them, his right hand on the one and his left hand on the other. And Samson said, "Let me die with the Philistines." Then he bowed with all his strength, and the house fell upon the lords and upon all the people who were in it. So the dead whom he killed at his death were more than those whom he had killed during his life.[4]

Samson died by suicide while seeking revenge on his enemy. He burned with hatred against the Philistines for blinding him, and in a rage brought down the coliseum, killing his enemy and himself.

So, the first two suicides were acts done by men who were mortally wounded and gave a reason for taking their own lives.

Samson's suicide was done in an act of war (and vengeance) against the enemy. Whether or not a person believes suicide is morally acceptable, at least we can understand the reason for their decision.

The other three suicides recorded in the Old Testament were men who were not mortally wounded, and from the information we have, they were physically healthy. Nor did they seek to avenge themselves. However, they all had something in common. In each instance, the biblical text says they "saw" something that led to suicide. Let's take a look at what each one saw.

First is Saul's armor-bearer. Immediately after Saul killed himself, his armor-bearer also died by suicide. Notice what the armor-bearer saw that prompted his suicide, "And when his armor-bearer *saw that Saul was dead*, he also fell upon his sword and died with him."[5] The armor-bearer saw that his king was dead and gave up hope. His hope was in King Saul and when his king was dead, he lost hope and ended his own life. *Hope should not be in a human relationship.*

Next is Ahithophel, the advisor to Absalom. Ahithophel, one of King David's advisors, became a co-conspirator when David's son Absalom usurped the throne. Absalom raised an army of rebels and captured the palace. David and those loyal to him fled Jerusalem to escape the rebel force. Ahithophel advised Absalom to continue the pursuit and attack while David was on the run. However, David sneaked his own man into Absalom's inner circle to offer counsel. David's man gave counsel contrary to Ahithophel and advised him to delay the attack. Absalom heeded the advice of the mole and when Ahithophel saw that his counsel was rejected, he killed himself. "When Ahithophel *saw that his counsel was not followed*, he saddled his donkey and went off home to his own city. He set his house in order and hanged himself, and he died and was buried in the tomb of his father."[6] When Ahithophel saw that his counsel was rejected, he lost hope and ended his own life. *Hope should not be in one's self.*

The last suicide recorded in the Old Testament is Zimri's. Zimri was a military commander and turncoat who murdered his own king (Elah) then took Israel's throne for himself. His reign was short-lived, only seven days. When other troops heard of the coup, they made Omri king and launched an attack on the capital city. When Zimri saw the city was overrun he killed himself. The account is found in 1 Kings, "And when Zimri *saw that the city was taken*, he went into the citadel of the king's house and burned the king's house over him with fire and died."[7] Zimri placed his hope in the protection of the city and when he saw it fall he lost hope and ended his own life. *Hope should not be in a place.*

There's only one suicide recorded in the New Testament, and it's one of the most famous suicides in human history—that of Judas Iscariot, the man who betrayed Jesus. Judas was one of Twelve called to be apostles and who followed Jesus for three years before his crucifixion. Of these twelve men, only Judas took his own life. All of the others, except John, became martyrs. John was exiled to a prison island where he lived out the remainder of his life. What was the difference between the one who died by suicide and the other eleven who faced imprisonment, torture, and horrible deaths?

Why did Judas opt for suicide? Was it because he betrayed Jesus? Was it because he could not be forgiven? Or was it something else? When we compare Judas' decision with the suicides recorded in the Old Testament, we find that Judas fits into the second category of physically healthy men who lost hope. To understand why Judas took his own life, we need to understand Judas. We need to know why he lost hope. In order to know why he lost hope, we need to know who or what he placed his hope in.

Judas is first mentioned when Jesus named his twelve apostles. Matthew, Mark, and Luke record the selection of the Twelve. Although the Gospel writers change the order of the names, Peter is always listed first and Judas Iscariot always last. Also, when each Gospel writer (including John) first introduce Judas, they present him as the traitor or betrayer. Here is Luke's record,

> In these days he [Jesus] went out to the mountain to pray, and all night he continued in prayer to God. And when day came, he called his disciples and chose from them twelve, whom he named apostles: Simon, whom he named Peter, and Andrew his brother, and James and John, and Philip, and Bartholomew, and Matthew, and Thomas, and James the son of Alphaeus, and Simon who was called the

Zealot, and Judas the son of James, and Judas Iscariot, who became a traitor.[8]

However, it's also important to note that none of the Gospel writers disparage Judas.[9] They simply present the facts surrounding his life and the actions he took. Judas was a popular Jewish name in the first century, in fact, there are five men named Judas in the New Testament. To distinguish individuals, people were often identified by their hometown, their father's name, or their occupation. Judas is identified as Judas Iscariot (a reference to his hometown in Judah)[10] and sometimes as the son of Simon. This distinguished him from the Apostle Judas the son of James as well as the other men named Judas in the New Testament. He was the only apostle from Judah, the other eleven were from Galilee, as was Jesus. Like many things about Judas, his occupation remains a mystery.

What we do know is this, he was a disciple of Jesus and specially chosen to be an apostle. It was common practice in first century Judaism for people to follow a rabbi or teacher and become a disciple or student of the rabbi. Normally, people chose to follow a rabbi and to learn from him. The goal was to eventually take the place of the rabbi and to become rabbis themselves. But Jesus was different. He chose his followers. Among the many early disciples, Jesus appointed twelve to be apostles. These were special messengers with authority to preach, teach, heal, and wield power over demonic forces. Judas was one of the chosen.

What were the apostles' expectations? Were they looking for their rabbi to be arrested, tried, and sentenced to death? Absolutely not! They were looking for the Messiah, the one promised by the Old Testament prophets to reestablish King David's throne in Jerusalem. They were looking for a king; and they expected to co-reign with him. Even when Jesus clearly told them—at least three times—that he was going to be arrested, tried, and condemned to death, they missed it. The apostles were so concerned about their own personal position and agenda, they missed what Jesus told them clearly. Look, "And he began to teach them that the Son of Man must suffer many things and be rejected by the elders and the chief priests and the scribes and be killed, and after three days rise again. And he said this plainly."[11]

He said it plainly and repeatedly, yet they didn't get it. They heard, but they didn't listen. In fact, Peter even rebuked Jesus for saying such things, "And Peter took him aside and began to rebuke him. But turning and seeing his disciples, he rebuked Peter and said, 'Get behind me, Satan! For you are not setting your mind on the things of God, but on the things of man.'" [12] What Jesus told Peter is crucial, "For you are not setting your mind on the things of God, but on the things of man." But Peter wasn't the only apostle who had set his mind on *the things of man*.

In his Gospel, Mark records three separate incidents when Jesus told the apostles that he was going to be arrested, convicted, and killed. The third time was just days before his crucifixion on the road from Jericho to Jerusalem. While approaching the Holy City where the temple stood and where Jesus would soon be hanged on the cross, James and John made a request of Jesus, "And James and John, the sons of Zebedee, came up to him and said to him, 'Teacher, we want you to do for us whatever we ask of you.' And he said to them, 'What do you want me to do for you?' And they said to him, 'Grant us to sit, one at your right hand and one at your left, in your glory.'"[13]

Peter, James, and John were the three apostles closest to Jesus. They made up the inner circle and were allowed to see things the others did not (i.e., the resurrection of Jairus' daughter and the Mount of Transfiguration). Yet, they didn't expect Jesus to be condemned to death and die on a Roman cross. If the apostles closest to Jesus didn't understand that Jesus was destined to the cross, we can expect the others didn't either. In fact, Mark says as much, "for he was teaching his disciples, saying to them, 'The Son of Man is going to be delivered into the hands of men, and they will kill him. And when he is killed, after three days he will rise.' But *they did not understand* the saying, and were afraid to ask him." [14]

Now, let's look a little more deeply into what Judas expected from Jesus. One thing to note is that he was close to Jesus, as mentioned, he was one of the Twelve specially chosen by Jesus. Although not part of the inner circle, Judas was likely closer to Jesus than most of the others. At the Last Supper Passover feast, he was next to Jesus, near enough for Jesus to hand him a piece of bread. He was also entrusted with the moneybag.

But Judas was also a thief. When Jesus and the apostles were in Bethany just six days before his arrest, Mary, the sister of Lazarus and Martha, anointed Jesus with expensive perfume. Judas objected, "Why was this ointment not sold for three hundred denarii and given to the poor?" This was a significant amount of money. Three hundred denarii were equivalent to a year's wages for a common laborer.[15] Judas' objection appeared legitimate on the surface. He seemed concerned for the poor and believed a better use of the perfume would be to sell it and give the money to the poor. But John provides further insight into the betrayer's motive, "He said this, not because he cared about the poor, but because he was a thief."[16]

Everyone has stolen something sometime in their life. Maybe it was cookies from the cookie jar, a pencil from a fellow student, or time from a boss. But there's a difference between stealing and being a thief. Being labeled a thief defines a person's character and reveals their heart. Jesus said, "For where your treasure is, there your heart will be also."[17] Judas was all about Judas, what he could get for himself.

Recall when Jesus said to Peter, "For you are not setting your mind on the things of God, but on the things of man"?[18] This was Judas' problem. Not only was his mind on the things of this world, so too was his hope. Like the other apostles, he expected Jesus to set up his throne in Jerusalem and release the Jews from Roman oppression. He didn't understand Jesus' kingdom is not of this world. When questioned by Pilate, Jesus said, "My kingdom is not of this world. If my kingdom were of this world, my servants would have been fighting, that I might not be delivered over to the Jews. But my kingdom is not from the world." [19]

Judas missed it. He allowed Satan to influence him and he opted with Satan over Jesus. "Then Satan entered into Judas called Iscariot, who was of the number of the twelve. He went away and conferred with the chief priests and officers how he might betray him to them."[20]

[Satan? "Do you believe Satan is real?" you ask. Yes, I do. Here's why, the Bible has proven to be reliable. Throughout history it has been critiqued, studied, researched, and checked for authenticity more than any other piece of written literature and has never been shown to be in error. Are there those who believe the Bible is full of myths and scientific inaccuracies? Yes, there are. But the Bible has yet to be proven wrong. Some come up with theories that contradict the Bible and if true, would discredit it. However, these theories haven't been proven true—they remain *theories*. It's dishonest to discount one theory (i.e., the biblical account) with another theory. Some choose to believe scientific theory; I choose to believe the Bible. Many scientific theories have proven to be wrong; the Bible has never been proven wrong. The Bible doesn't contradict any scientific law of nature. In fact, the Bible has proven to be accurate when science and historians thought otherwise. But this book isn't an apologetic book on the Bible. J. Warner Wallace does a good job defending the biblical text and the supernatural in *Cold-Case Christianity*. Also, keep in mind, the place where we learn about Satan is the same place we learn about God.]

So, because Satan entered into Judas, does that mean Judas is not responsible for his own actions? No, that's not what it means. Judas made the decision to betray his friend. The text says that Judas met with the chief priests and agreed with them to lead them to Jesus. Further, Judas wasn't the only apostle whom Satan influenced. Jesus called Peter "Satan" when Peter rebuked him. Later the Apostle Paul wrote to believers in Ephesus,

And you were dead in the trespasses and sins in which you once walked, following the course of this world, *following the prince of the power of the air* [Satan], the spirit that is now at work in the sons of disobedience—among whom we all once lived in the passions of our flesh, carrying out the desires of the body and the mind.[21]

That's what Judas did. He *followed the prince of the power of the air*

(Satan) and was *carrying out the desires of the body and the mind*. Hope gives meaning to life, and Judas' hope was to be an important player in Jesus' earthly kingdom. Judas went to the chief priests and agreed to betray Jesus for thirty pieces of silver, "And they were glad, and agreed to give him money. So he consented and sought an opportunity to betray him to them in the absence of a crowd."[22] No one made him. It was his choice to do so, and he did. He did because that was his hope. Here's how one scholar addressed the issue:

> Satan thus "targets" some individuals, especially those close to Jesus or the Christian mission, for uniquely diabolical purposes. These initiatives should not be understood as irresistible, for none of those targeted is absolved of guilt. Judas is not "possessed" by Satan in the sense that he cannot do otherwise, nor does Satan *cause* Judas, Peter, or Ananias and Sapphira to sin. Each individual remains responsible for his or her moral failure.[23]

Hence, Judas was responsible for his betrayal of Jesus. This begs the question, "If he wanted to be part of Jesus' earthly kingdom, why did Judas betray him?" The Bible doesn't explicitly say, but the two prevailing positions are that he did it for the money or he did it to force Jesus' hand into setting up the kingdom immediately. As we have seen, the Bible describes Judas as both a thief and traitor. Let's consider both.

A thief is after money, and Judas agreed to turn Jesus over for money. Is it possible that this was his ultimate motive? Possibly, but not likely. Thirty pieces of silver was the equivalent of about four months wages.[24] That's a significant amount. But if that was his goal, he got what he wanted. So, why did he return the money and choose to die by suicide? "Then when Judas, his betrayer, saw that Jesus was condemned, he changed his mind and brought back the thirty pieces of silver to the chief priests and the elders."[25]

Judas confessed to the Jewish leaders that Jesus was innocent and then he hanged himself, "'I have sinned by betraying innocent blood.' They said, 'What is that to us? See to it yourself.' And throwing down the pieces of silver into the temple, he departed, and he went and hanged himself."[26] Did Judas hang himself out of remorse for being part of a conspiracy to kill an innocent man, or was it out of remorse that he wouldn't get what he wanted from Jesus?

Judas changed his mind when he *saw that Jesus was condemned.* Apparently, Judas didn't expect Jesus to be condemned to die. Neither did the other apostles. In fact, none of Jesus' many followers expected him to be condemned to death. So, what did Judas expect? I believe he expected Jesus to be found innocent and for the Jewish leaders to accept that Jesus was the Messiah. That is what Jesus claimed and what the apostles believed. Being found innocent by the Jewish Sanhedrin would vindicate him, rally public support, and open the way for him to become Israel's King. But when Judas saw that Jesus was condemned to die, he lost hope.

Saul's armorer-bearer, Ahithophel, Zimri, and Judas all took their own lives because they lost hope. The armor-bearer's hope was in King Saul. Ahithophel's hope was in his own wisdom. Zimri's hope was in the protection the city provided. Judas' hope was in his own idea of Jesus' kingdom.

Hope is why we live. When hope is lost, all is lost. It's that simple.

4

HOPE GIVES LIFE MEANING

Hope springs eternal in the human breast.
—Alexander Pope

Hope begins early in life. From early childhood we're always looking forward to something with great anticipation. Something more. Something new. Something better. Toddlers look forward to daddy coming home, a popsicle with mom, or going to grandma's house. Children anticipate the next exciting thing, a trip to Disney World, summer camp, Christmas, or their birthday. Teens can't wait to start high school, get a driver's license, or go on their first date. Young adults look forward to college, trade school, a career, or marriage. The next thing you know, they're looking forward to children, a promotion, and retirement. Then it's grandchildren, traveling the country, or spending time enjoying a hobby. Always hoping for more, for new, for better.

I was no different, and like the other kids I grew up with, I could hardly wait for Christmases, birthdays, starting school, finishing school, my first bicycle, job, and car. Adulthood didn't change things all that much. I looked forward to entering the military, then being discharged from the military. But, more than anything, I looked with great anticipation to the day I'd be sworn in as a police officer.

A lot of high schoolers I talk with today have no idea what career path they want to pursue. Some do, but when asked what they want for a career the majority give the same answer, "I don't know." That wasn't me. I knew from early childhood what I wanted to spend my life doing. No doubt the television shows of the 1960s and 70s influenced my desire. Television transported me into the past with shows like *Gunsmoke, The Wild, Wild West,* and *Bonanza,* while *Star Trek* transported me into the future. But shows that really put a longing in me were the police shows: *Adam-12, Columbo,* and *Hawaii Five-O* (the original series!). Cops and robbers, good guys and bad guys, heroes and villains intrigued me. From the time I can recall all I wanted to do was to be a police officer. Actually, I really wanted to be a lawman in the old West, but I knew I couldn't go back in time, so policing in modern-day America was my only real option. I grew up with the hope of one day being a police officer.

F riday, December 9th, 1983, was that day. The day I imagined my whole life—police academy graduation day. On that Friday, the San Antonio Police Academy graduated Cadet class 83-B and San Antonio had 33 new police officers chomping at the bit—I was one. I was assigned to the 3-11 shift, specifically to the downtown one section. The next day I started the two-week on-the-job training program. For the first two weeks of my new career, I was assigned to Field Training Officer Bobby Spicer. Spicer worked district 1-4, and over those fourteen days we handled a variety of calls. Everything from shoplifters, to public intoxication arrests, to sexual assault reports, and even a disturbance for a man with a hand-grenade!

Christmas Day, 1983 should have been the best of my twenty-two Christmases. I finished the field training program and was going to be by myself in a blue and white police cruiser, patrolling the streets of downtown San Antonio. But it was a somber Christmas afternoon. The 3-11 Roll Call wasn't the usual cutting up and teasing. Officers were quiet and kept to themselves. A roll of black electrical tape was being passed around. I cut off a piece with my Buck® knife and passed it on. I unpinned my badge and ran the tape across the middle, covering up the number 817. I pinned the badge back on my chest. The black tape over our badge numbers was our way to remember and honor Officer Gilbert Ramirez who was shot and killed the night before. The lieutenant walked from the patrol office onto the stage. There were no general orders read. No BOLOs. No snide remarks. No jokes. He placed the clipboard on the lectern, and with a melancholy voice said, "Roll Call."

"White."

"Here, sir."

"One-one."

"Rios."

"Here, sir."

"One-two."

He continued. Then called my name, "Rupp."

"Here, sir."

"One-six."

After giving the last district assignment, he looked across the room at the silent officers and said, "Be careful." He walked off the stage and everyone headed for the stairs. There was a job to do.

Regular district officers had their own set of keys to the district car, relief officers had to grab a set of keys from the key box to the district they were assigned to that day. Ironically, I drew 1-6, the same district I rode on my first cadet ride. Only this time I was solo. I found my car in the parking lot. It was a well-used 1982 Dodge Diplomat. I climbed in, unlocked the radio, turned the engine on, adjusted the seat and mirrors, and seat-belted in my briefcase on the passenger side of the bench seat.

The radio was on the proper channel, I turned it on, and adjusted the volume. Radio chatter came through the speaker from 3-11 officers checking in service, daylight officers asking for case numbers, and dispatchers assigning calls.

Exiting the parking lot, I turned left into Graham alley, then right onto S. Flores Street, I reached toward the dash, slipped the mic from the clip, held it next to my mouth, and trying to sound calm and confident checked in service, "10-8, 1-6."

Immediately the dispatcher responded, "1-6, make 411 Barrera. Possible DOA." "DOA" stands for dead-on-arrival, and we used the acronym as a substitute for the word *dead*.

"10-4, 1-6. Did they give an apartment number?"

"Negative. The complainant said there's a man on the second-floor landing, he's unresponsive."

"10-4," I said and replaced the mic. I jotted down the address, pulled over, and found the address in my street guide. That was my first call and I'll likely never forget it. It turned out to be a down-and-out drunk, not a DOA. I called for Emergency Medical Service. The paramedics checked him out and determined he was fine, just drunk. I booked him for public intoxication and checked back into service. Thus, began my career on the SAPD.

Policing didn't disappoint. It promised to be a great career and provide a decent income. But it wasn't an end all. I didn't stop hoping, dreaming, and anticipating. No one does, there's always something else—something elusive. I wanted to marry and have a family. In 1986, I met and married Sherry Lynn James. A couple years later, Sherry became pregnant with our first child. We were excited, Sherry started planning for what she needed, what color to paint the nursery, and all the other things first-time moms-to-be plan. I started thinking about being a father and everything that will mean. Will it be a boy or a girl? What name will we choose? We were both excited and filled with hope about the new life coming into our lives.

Sherry was three months along, and I was hunting in the Texas Hill Country when I received the news. Her father showed up at camp—Sherry lost the baby. We don't know why. She had a miscarriage and just like that it was over. It hit Sherry pretty hard and I did my best to comfort her. Family, friends, and several ladies from our church family also reached out to Sherry. I was surprised by how much the miscarriage affected me. I felt a deep loss and had no answers for myself or my wife. I didn't know why. I still don't. But life went on, and with it hope. Everyone goes through dark days in life. For some the days are longer and darker. The light of hope brings us out of the darkness.

Hope is anticipating. Hope is expecting. Hope is believing. Hope is so important that when people lose it, they cease living. Some continue to exist, but aren't really living, they are just existing. Some even choose to end their life. While I write this chapter, the world is in the midst of the 2020 COVID 19 pandemic. Experts say the suicide rate is expected to increase because of widespread fear. A 50-year-old man from India was reported to be the first suicide related death to the pandemic. Here's what an article from *Scientific American* said:

[The man] kept watching coronavirus-related videos and became convinced he had the virus and would infect his family: he was a victim of panic contagion. Panic can demoralize us, it can paralyze us with paranoia and fear, and these emotions in turn lead to hopelessness and desperation.[1]

The bottom line is "hopelessness." The article said he was a victim of "panic contagion" but in reality, he was a victim of hopelessness. Panic didn't result in suicide. His loss of hope did. When he felt there was no hope, he ended his life. Viktor Frankl said of himself and his fellow prisoners in the Nazi concentration camps, "The thought of suicide was entertained by nearly everyone, if only for a brief time. It was born of the hopelessness of the situation."[2]

Why is hope so important? Because hope gives life meaning. Hope gives us a purpose. Hope gives us a reason to go on. Frankl warned of a twentieth century phenomenon he dubbed the *existential vacuum*. He said that the existential vacuum is a void of purpose in a person's life that is marked by boredom, and warned that, "Not a few cases of suicide can be traced back to this existential vacuum."[3] Frankl believed that humans have a purpose greater than themselves and that each life has meaning beyond him or herself. When a person either loses sight of that meaning or never discovers it, there is a danger of losing hope. Frankl advised that, "[I]f therapists wish to foster their patients' mental health, they should not be afraid to create a sound amount of tension through a reorientation toward the meaning of one's life."[4] Hence, this is the reason he wrote *Man's Search for Meaning*. For Frankl, life meant more than seeking pleasure, avoiding pain, and procreating (to prevent humanity from extinction). He believed a person's life has meaning beyond the individual. Frankl believed that even in the midst of suffering life has meaning.

Surprisingly, not everyone wants life to have meaning. The successful author and screen writer Aldous Huxley (1894-1963) was such a person. He wrote the celebrated *A Brave New World*, one of the best-selling novels of the twentieth century. But, in his book *Ends and Means* he said that life has no meaning beyond a personal agenda. While I disagree with him, his blatant honesty is admirable. He wrote,

> I had motives for not wanting the world to have a meaning; and consequently assumed that it had none, and was able without any difficulty to find satisfying reasons for this assumption. The philosopher who finds no meaning in the world is not concerned exclusively with a problem in pure metaphysics. He is also concerned to prove that there is no valid reason why he personally should not do as he wants to do. For myself, as no doubt for most of my friends, the philosophy of meaninglessness was essentially an instrument of liberation from a certain system of morality. We objected to the morality because it interfered with our sexual freedom. The supporters of this system claimed that it embodied the meaning—the Christian meaning, they insisted—of the world. There was one admirably simple method of confuting these people and justifying ourselves in our erotic revolt: we would deny that the world had any meaning whatever.[5]

Huxley chose to believe life has no meaning because he didn't want it to. Meaning for him was fulfillment of his personal selfish desires, therefore he dismissed a meaning of life beyond one's self.

When all of a person's hope is on *the things of man*, i.e., temporary pleasure and comfort, hope is easily lost. With technology and automation, Americans are blessed (or perhaps cursed) with more free time to do what we want. We are blessed in that we have more time to do the things that bring us enjoyment. The problem is, we find that these don't bring lasting contentment. So, we pursue something else. We buy new toys, start new hobbies, and go to new places to fulfill that elusive yearning that's deep inside each of us, the yearning that's not satisfied by career, marriage, or entertainment.

Frankl wrote of this mysterious longing in his 1984 Postscript to *Man's Search for Meaning*. He entitled the addendum "The Case for a Tragic Optimism," and said that the key is to remain optimistic even in the face of three tragic realities that are common to all. He called these three woes the *triad of tragedy*. They are pain, guilt, and death. While most Americans seek to avoid, mask, or deny these realities, Frankl looked for their meaning.

He observed that the American culture demands personal happiness. He is right, even in our Declaration of Independence we state that one of our unalienable rights is the pursuit of happiness. Hence, we've come to believe that happiness is a right (not its pursuit) and that we are to attain it no matter the price. So, we try. We seek happiness in hobbies, careers, money, and relationships. While we may experience happiness for a time, it is too soon gone. Frankl writes, "[H]appiness cannot be pursued; it must ensue. One must have a reason to 'be happy.' ...a human being is not one in pursuit of happiness but rather in search of a reason to become happy."[6]

Again, Frankl is right. Happiness depends on happenings. If something we regard as good happens, it makes us happy. We enjoy the pleasure happiness brings so we pursue it like a drug, doing whatever we can to get that "happiness high." But Frankl was realistic. He knew everyone will experience pain, guilt, and death. None of these realities are pleasurable and they don't make us happy, so we do what we can to avoid, or at least delay them.

Although Frankl makes some very important points about life's meaning, I disagree with where his search for meaning ends. Like many do, he too fell prey to setting his mind *on the things of man*. So, what were his answers to the triad of tragedy: pain, guilt, and death? Here's what he wrote,

[W]hat matters is to make the best of any given situation. "The best," however, is that which the Latin called *optimum*—hence the reason I speak of a tragic optimism, that is, an optimism in the face of tragedy and in view of the human potential which at its best always allows for: (1) turning suffering into a human achievement and accomplishment; (2) deriving from guilt the opportunity to change oneself for the better; and (3) deriving from life's transitoriness [certain end in death] an incentive to take responsible action.[7]

Frankl's search for meaning found himself where he started, with man. He spoke of human potential, achievement, self-betterment, and responsibility. But is that it? Does it all ultimately end here, in this world? No, because even personal achievement, moral living, and philanthropy do not fulfill the mysterious yearning deep inside each of us. These things may bring us temporary relief, but the yearning remains. Why is there an emptiness deep inside that we seek to fill? Where does that yearning come from? Why do we believe it can be filled? This mysterious yearning and the hope that it can be satisfied come from the same place, from within. C.S. Lewis wrote about this elusive yearning and says many try to silence it.

Almost our whole education has been directed to silencing this shy, persistent, inner voice; almost all our modern philosophies have been devised to convince us that the good of man is to be found on this earth. And yet it is a remarkable thing that such philosophies of Progress or Creative Evolution themselves bear reluctant witness to the truth that our real goal is elsewhere.[8]

The wise King Solomon wrote, "He [God] has made everything beautiful in its time. Also, he has put eternity into man's heart, yet so that he cannot find out what God has done from the beginning to the end."[9] What does it mean that God put eternity in our hearts? It means that the desire for more, new, and better and the hope they can be attained comes from our hearts. It means that we believe things should be better. We hope for more, for new, for better. We long for a utopian society. This longing is reflected in Anne Murray's 1983 hit song *A Little Good News*:

There's a local paper rolled up in a rubber band
   One more sad story's one more than I can stand
   Just once how I'd like to see the headline say
   "Not much to print today, can't find nothin' bad to say," because
   Nobody robbed a liquor store on the lower part of town
   Nobody OD'ed, nobody burned a single buildin' down
   Nobody fired a shot in anger, nobody had to die in vain
   We sure could use a little good news today[10]

But it goes deeper than more, new, and better. More isn't enough, we long for *forever*.[11] New isn't the answer, it's *all things new*.[12] Better isn't sufficient, we long for *perfection*.[13] We long for more than a world without corruption. We long for a perfect world. Why? Because God put eternity in our hearts. When we think of this, we think of the future. A never-ending future. But eternity includes the past. When God created the world, he made "everything beautiful in its time." Adam and Eve were created in a perfect world. A world without pain, guilt, and death. Like human DNA, this longing is imprinted in our hearts. The human craving is for that world to be restored. For humanity's relationship with God to be reconciled. For things to be as they were intended.

That's why man's search for meaning goes beyond himself, it goes beyond humanity, it reaches out to God. The very best we can do falls short. Lewis agrees, "Do what we will, then, we remain conscious of a desire which no natural happiness will satisfy."[14] This yearning is a spiritual hunger that cannot be satisfied by the physical, the mental, or the things of man.

In further comment on this yearning, Lewis said, "[I]f we are made for heaven, the desire for our proper place will be already in us."[15] He continues and admits that which we search for is elusive because "it is a desire for something that has never actually appeared in our experience."[16] We long to live forever, yet—physically—we are finite beings. We long for a world without pain, but such a world is outside of our experience. We long for perfection, but we've never experienced perfection. Lewis refers to the search for perfection as "beauty" and says that we search for it *in* the arts but it is *through* the arts that this longing is sparked.

> We cannot hide it because our experience is constantly suggesting it, and we betray ourselves like lovers at the mention of a name. Our commonest expedient is to call it beauty and behave as if that had settled the matter.
>
> The books or the music in which we thought the beauty was located will betray us if we trust to them; it was not *in* them, it only came *through* them, and what came through them was longing. These things—the beauty, the memory of our own past—are good images of what we really desire; but if they are mistaken for the thing itself they turn into dumb idols, breaking the hearts of their worshippers.[17]

The inner, elusive yearning that is common to all humanity is a spiritual thirst that can only be quenched spiritually. There is more to humanity than a physical body and a mind capable of reason. There is a spiritual aspect that longs for perfection. A hope for perfection that can only be found in God.

5

FAITH IN PEOPLE

There were many dark moments when my faith in humanity was sorely tested.
—Nelson Mandela

There are bad people in this world. There always have been and some of the worst have risen to lead nations—Stalin, Hitler, Pol Pot, Ivan the Terrible, Genghis Khan, and Atila the Hun, to name a few. Others didn't rise to national leadership but prowled the streets and countrysides of our world, including people like Luis Garvito who is suspected of murdering more than 300 children in South America. In America we have murderers like Ted Bundy, John Wayne Gacy, Charles Manson, and the numerous mass murderers who have shot up schools, churches, shopping malls, theaters, and concerts in recent years.

On the other hand, there are good people in this world. There always have been and some of the best have risen to lead nations— Cyrus II, Augustus Caesar, Queen Elizabeth I, George Washington, and Abraham Lincoln are often cited. Others didn't rise to national leadership but walked among us. People like Jonas Salk, who invented the polio vaccine at great personal cost, America's Civil Rights leader Martin Luther King, Jr., the Catholic Nun Mother Teresa who served Calcutta's poor, and many other not-so-famous people whom we personally know.

Knowing that the world is made up of both naughty and nice begs the question, "Are human beings inherently good or inherently bad?" Policing in America tends to sway a person's opinion of humanity. The streets have a way of hitting officers in the face with a dose of reality.

~

At twenty-two and freshly out of the Air Force, I didn't have much life experience. Little did I know that I was about to experience life as I'd never seen it on the streets of San Antonio. As mentioned in an earlier chapter, the first night riding as a police cadet my training officer and I responded to a call for a disturbance with a gun that turned out to be a murder. Although there are plenty of serious violent crime calls in any major metropolitan area, domestic disturbances are, by far, the most common calls-for-service. They also shed light on the sinister side of humanity.

Having been raised in what was considered a stable American family, I was ignorant of the abuse and violence that is found in many American homes. In the Air Force I saw very little domestic violence. Not because it didn't exist, but because dependent spouses (generally wives) knew that if they reported an abusive military spouse it might mean the end of a career. My first year on the SAPD, I was assigned to the downtown "one-section" on the 3-11 shift. At the time, the section was bordered by several highways. However, there was a small area on the near westside that was part of the one-section. Most of this area was government-subsidized housing projects. In the early 1980s, virtually all of the housing in the one-section was either government-subsidized or neighborhoods where low-income families lived. These families were primarily Hispanic. Hence, much of my first experience policing was making calls for family disturbances to low-income Hispanic families. It surprised me how many men got drunk and abused their families, either physically, mentally, or both—but my education had just begun.

In late 1984, I was transferred to the seven-section, on San Antonio's northeast side. The seven-section covered a very large area. The city was growing, and leadership simply made the districts larger, encompassing more land and more people, but still served by the same number of officers. About a year or so after my transfer, the administration decided to redistrict the entire city. We went from seven sections to ten. The seven-section was downsized and became the eleven-section (there was no ten-section, it would confuse our 10-code communication). After the shake-up, I remained on the 3-11 shift and ended up in the new eleven-section, with my own district, 11-4. The district was bordered by Perrin-Beitel Road on the west, Loop 410 on the south, Thousand Oaks Drive on the north, and IH 35 on the east. Although primarily Caucasian, the demographics were much more diverse from the one-section.

Guess what I learned—the calls were the same. I was far busier, and generally calls were waiting when I checked in service. It was common to make twenty or more calls in an eight-hour shift. But, like the one-section, the vast majority of calls were for family disturbances. There were low-income, middle-income, and upper-income living in my district, and I made calls for drunks abusing their family members from every class of citizen. Ethnicity, education, and money didn't make a difference—men (and even women) from all walks of life got drunk and abused their families, either physically, mentally, or both. Makes one think humanity is inherently evil—my education continued.

One warm summer day in 1985, the dispatcher called my number before I had a chance to check 10-8 (into service and available for calls). I was still in the parking lot transferring equipment from by personal vehicle to my police cruiser when I got the call.

"11-4, are you by the radio," the dispatcher asked.

"10-4, getting ready to check in," I said.

"11-4 make [address] for a possible stabbing. Use caution, no cover available."

Well, I guess I was in service. "10-4, 11-4, I'm on the way."

I looked up the address in the street guide and found it was in the Sun Gate subdivision, right about in the middle of my district, 13 miles from downtown. I put on my seatbelt, flipped the toggle switch to my overhead lights, jumped on IH 35 northbound, and pushed accelerator pedal on the '84 Ford Crown Victoria to the floor. She responded and I drifted to the left lane. We rarely used our sirens on the highway, with the speed, wind noise, rolled-up windows, air conditioners, and radios blasting people didn't hear it anyway. It wasn't rush hour, but traffic was heavy at 3 p.m. What was normally a twenty-minute drive, running code-two took about twelve to fourteen. I took the ramp to NE Loop 410, exited at Perrin-Beitel, and turned north. I activated the siren and wove through heavy traffic for a mile, then turned right on Sun Gate, and into the subdivision. So as not to alert any suspects that still might be in the area, I turned off the siren and overhead lights. A couple blocks into the subdivision, I pulled up in front of a middle-class residence in the normally quiet and peaceful neighborhood.

I stepped out of the blue and white and keyed the radio, "11-4, I'm 10-6 (on scene)."

"10-4, 11-4, let me know what you have."

A frantic woman ran up and told me she found the front door to her neighbor's house open. She knocked and called out to anyone inside. When there was no response she went in and saw the body of a female lying face down in a pool of blood. She ran out and called the police.

"Did you see anyone else inside?" I asked.

"No."

"Did anyone leave?"

"No, I didn't see anyone."

"Okay, wait here," I said and notified dispatch, "11-4, I have a report of one victim in the house, unknown suspects. I'm going inside."

"10-4, use caution. All officers hold the air," she responded, instructing other officers not to tie-up the radio until I cleared the house.

I drew my service revolver, approached the door, and announced,

"Police!" No response. Using tactics learned from the police academy, I stepped through the door and started to clear the house. The living room was clear, as was the kitchen. I started down the hallway, the door at the end was open. I paused to listen. All was quiet. Cautiously, I checked the side rooms. I was trained never to leave a room uncleared behind me. The rooms were clear. When I reached the master bedroom, I stepped into the room and quickly scanned it from left to right. The bed was on the left, to the right was the master bath. Face down, on the linoleum floor lay the body of a Hispanic female in her mid-thirties. Blood covered the floor where she lay. Multiple puncture wounds were in her back; defensive wounds on her arms and hands. The walls and mirror were splashed with blood. I checked the closet and cleared the room. It was clear—no suspects to be found.

The female was obviously deceased, but officers couldn't make that call. I notified dispatch, "11-4, start me EMS, and notify 11-0 (my sergeant) and Homicide."

"10-4, 11-4."

Written in blood across the bathroom mirror was "REDRUM."[1] "Murder" spelled backwards. *What type of person was capable of such evil?* The follow-up investigation by homicide revealed a 15-year-old, white male neighbor was responsible. In a matter of days, detectives secured a search warrant, located the murder weapon at his house, and made an arrest.

You can start to see why police officers become cynical and distrusting of their fellow humans.

What about the question I asked at the beginning of this chapter, "Are human beings inherently good or inherently bad?" Let's take a look at what some great thinkers through history believed.

Moses (1526-1406 BC), the Hebrew prophet and patriarch, is credited with writing the first five books of the Jewish scriptures, which Christians accept as the first books of the Old Testament. In Genesis

Moses wrote about humanity's bent, "The Lord saw that the wickedness of man was great in the earth, and that every intention of the thoughts of his heart was only evil continually."[2]

King Solomon (989-931 BC) Israel's third king, who is regarded as a man of peace and the wisest person who has lived said this about mankind, "Surely there is not a righteous man on earth who does good and never sins."[3] Sin can be defined as "any failure to conform to the moral law of God in act, attitude, or nature."[4] Hence, sin goes beyond breaking established human law to breaking God's moral law.

The early Greek philosopher Plato (427-347 BC) believed that humans were self-centered, contentious, and evil. He said, "There is in every one of us, even those who seem to be most moderate, a type of desire that is terrible, wild, and lawless."[5] Because of their bent toward lawlessness, Plato believed humans must submit to the law of the state. He feared if people were left to themselves, there would be chaos in the streets because individuals always seek to satisfy their own appetite without much regard for the concerns of others.[6]

The Roman African, St. Augustine of Hippo (354-430), asserted that each person is afflicted with what he called "original sin" sometimes called "inherited sin." He wrote "[T]he deliberate sin of the first man is the cause of original sin".[7] Original sin is the Christian doctrine that Adam's disobedience in the Garden of Eden caused a "sin nature" to be passed down. No doubt the first century writings of the Apostle Paul influenced Augustine's position. Paul wrote, "Therefore, just as sin came into the world through one man [Adam], and death through sin, and so death spread to all men because all sinned."[8]

This naturally sparks the question, "If the doctrine of original sin is true, does this mean that individuals are not responsible for their own sin?" Augustine answered, "There can be no sin that is not voluntary, the learned and the ignorant admit this evident truth."[9] As a Christian theologian, Augustine obviously leaned heavily on his understanding of the Bible to support his position. The Bible points out that everyone has sinned, "For there is no distinction: for all have sinned."[10] Further, the Bible says that each person is personally responsible for their own sin, "He [God] will render to each one according to his works"[11] and "For the wrongdoer will be paid back for the wrong he has done, and there is no partiality."[12]

The seventeenth century English philosopher Thomas Hobbes (1588-1679) also believed humanity was basically evil and could only be controlled by legitimate government and a system of moral law. Hence, Hobbes believed in a strong state government to control behavior and prevent social disorder and anarchy.[13]

The German philosopher Immanuel Kant (1724-1804) believed that humans decide between moral and immoral choices. He believed that unlike animals, humans are not wholly determined to act by natural impulse neither are humans free of non-rational impulse.[14] Hence, we each make choices between right and wrong.

These great minds had a dire view of humanity.

More recently, some have come to believe that humanity is basically good. In fact, they say, we are inherently good and moral beings that become corrupted by our environment. Bad behavior is learned, they claim. A 2012 study indicates that people have a disposition to help others, even at personal cost.[15] However, this study simply affirms that humans have a moral compass that guides decisions based on benevolence. In other words, by nature there is a spark of good in humans. This study was touted by many media outlets that we are by nature morally good.

Perhaps the father of this thought is the French philosopher Jean-Jacques Rousseau (1712-1778) who alleged that science and philosophy contributed to humanity's depravity. He believed that by nature man is good and anything that is unnatural corrupts humanity from his natural moral state.[16] I believe Rousseau was on to something. According to the Bible, humanity was created without sin. Hence, by nature, we were created as moral beings. But when Adam chose to disobey God and eat the forbidden fruit, sin corrupted what was naturally good. This explains our bipolar morality of good and bad and explains why humanity is capable of both benevolence and evil.

Those who don't believe in a moral God have a problem explaining where morality comes from. Survival of the fittest doesn't explain moral decisions to save and care for those who can't contribute to society.

> "Where morality comes from is a really hard problem," says Alison Gopnik, a developmental psychologist at the University of California at Berkeley. "There isn't a moral module that is there innately. But the elements that underpin morality—altruism, sympathy for others, the understanding of other people's goals—are in place much earlier than we thought, and clearly in place before children turn 2."[17]

The conclusion must be that humans are capable of both moral goodness and moral depravity. With regard to good and bad, it appears that by nature, we're all morally bipolar. Perhaps, singer and songwriter, Waylon Jennings was on to something when he sang,

> There're two sides to me, and they ain't even friends
> > All sides are rising and there ain't no in between
> > When I'm bad I'm bad
> > When I'm good I'm the best you ever seen[18]

So, what does the inherent moral goodness or moral depravity of individuals have to do with a book about law enforcement officers and other warriors taking their own lives? It has to do where one places his or her faith.

Faith = hope.

Faith is something we all have. We live our lives by faith. We have faith the alarm clock will sound, we have faith our car will start, and we have faith the friend we planned to meet will be at the restaurant. Sometimes we are let down. The alarm clock doesn't sound. The car fails to start. Our friend forgets to show. Does this mean we stop depending on alarm clocks to wake us, cars to transport us, or friends to meet us? No. We understand sometimes things happen. But sometimes we need a new clock, car, or maybe even a new friend.

The question isn't whether or not we have faith, the question is,

"What do we have faith in?" Where we place our faith is foundational to how we live life and interpret our experiences.

A solid foundation is crucial. A house may look good from the outside, but if it's built on a shaky foundation it's only a matter of time before it comes crashing down. It's the same with us, a solid foundation is crucial. A foundation must support everything that is built on top of it. So, what type of foundation do we need? What makes for a solid foundation? We've already discussed that we are made up of a body, soul, and spirit—the physical, mental, and spiritual. Which one of these three is foundational to the other two?

Our foundation is clearly not our physical body. The body doesn't act on its own accord. In fact, if we listened to our bodies we'd be in trouble. My body tells me not to go for a run, to eat more chocolate, and do any number of other things that makes my body feel good. But my mind tells my body to exercise, limit the intake of chocolate, and to be careful about my physical activities.

So, should the mind be our foundation? After all, that's where we reason. We learn exercise is good for the body. Even if it causes the body to be uncomfortable, proper exercise will help the body to get into and keep in better shape. It also informs the body not to eat too much junk food, even if it tastes good, because junk food doesn't help the body to be healthy. The mind also warns us about unsafe physical activities.

But it's the spirit that holds our beliefs and informs our moral choices. When I entered the house where I believed a homicide occurred and where a suspect might be hiding, my mind reasoned, "There might be a bad guy in there who can hurt the body, don't go!"

However, the spirit said, "There might be a person in there who needs my help. Further, there might be a bad guy in there that's a threat to other people. You've sworn to serve and protect, so you're obligated to go in."

"Okay I'm going," I respond, choosing ethics over reason.

"Be careful. Use good tactics," the mind reminds me.

"That's reasonable," I agree.

Our core beliefs form our foundation. At the core is a person's theology. *Theology—are you serious?* Yes. One scholar said, "Theology is for everyone. Indeed, everyone needs to be a theologian."[19] What you believe about God shapes your core beliefs and is foundational to how you live. Belief about God spans the spectrum. It goes from the declared atheist who doesn't believe a god exists, to the agnostic who isn't sure (but leaves the door open), to the believer in God, or at least some supreme spiritual power.

According to a 2018 Gallup poll, 87% of Americans respond "Yes" when asked, "Do you believe in God?" The numbers drop to 79% when the question is worded differently, such as "Is God something you believe in?" or "Are you convinced God exists?" However, still well over two-thirds of Americans believe in God, and most (64%) say they are convinced God exists.[20]

Although the vast majority of Americans claim to believe in God, that's not where they place their faith. They may say they do, because that's what they are expected to say. But that's not the way they live. Most Americans place their faith in humanity. It may be themselves or others. Then, as a last resort, they turn to God. When they've tried everything else and nothing has worked, they ask God to help them.

Law enforcement officers are no different. As children and young adults, they grew up in an America that places their faith in fellow citizens. They grow up believing most people are good, honest, and strive to do no harm. Then the reality of policing hits them. When I worked Homicide, I can't recall the number of times I heard, "He (or she) would never kill anyone." Homicide detectives know better. Anyone is capable of murder.

Combat veterans see what humans are capable of in war. When one's faith is in humanity, the reality of policing destroys that foundation. When our foundation is weak, eventually the house will come down, and with it hope.

6

FAITH IN SOCIETIES, SYSTEMS, AND SCIENCE

Those who pay regard to vain idols forsake their hope of steadfast love.
—Jonah 2:8

Hope is why we live. Faith is why we hope. Faith is a foundation framed by beliefs. Faith is important—all important. There are two basic kinds of faith: *emotion-based* faith and *evidence-based* faith. Emotion-based faith is believing something because we want it to be true (or not believing something because we don't want it to be true). Evidence-based faith is believing something because there is evidence that supports the belief.

On January 6, 1995, at about 5:30 p.m., patrol officers notified the SAPD Homicide Office that they were at a house where two young children died under suspicious circumstances. The Dalton and Gutierrez families lived together at a rented house in the 100 block of East Magnolia Avenue, just north of downtown San Antonio. Sergeant Ray Torres, Detectives Jimmy Holguin, Dave Evans, and I responded. When we arrived, officers reported that the Dalton family lived upstairs and the Gutierrez family downstairs, and that both bodies were found downstairs. I entered the residence and found five-month-old Timothy Gutierrez lying on the couch, face-up, fully clothed. There appeared to be levity in his face and his body was cold to the touch. Two-year-old Rene Alicia Gutierrez was found in a make-shift bedroom. She was on a bed, lying on her right side, wearing only a diaper. There were fluid stains on a sheet next to her face. At her feet was a pillow that also appeared to have some type of bodily fluid on it. It looked dry, but a fly was attracted to it.

The living conditions were deplorable. Here's part of what I wrote in my report,

> The entire house was filthy. The living conditions were unsanitary. There appeared to be food smeared on the walls of the house. Dirty clothes were found throughout every room in the house. Both of the deceased children appeared to be dirty and unkept. Both children had wax build up in their ears from not being cleaned.[1]

At the residence were three adult women (sisters Patricia and Kathline Dalton, and a friend, Kellie Parker) and twelve-year-old Victoria, Patricia's daughter. The parents of the children were not present; they reportedly caught a bus and were across town shopping. They left their children in the care of the Daltons. The paramedics had no explanation, nor did any of the witnesses. We searched the house and looked for a cause of death. We checked for gas leaks or anything else that may have resulted in the death of two young children. We didn't know if the cause was natural, accidental, or homicide. Natural was not likely. Other than hygiene issues, the children appeared healthy. For one healthy child to suddenly die of natural causes was unlikely, for two it was extremely unlikely. Accidental death was possible, but how? And why only the children? Although not necessary to charge, detectives look for motive. Who benefits from the death? Our immediate suspicions went to the parents.

After finishing up at the scene, we returned to the Homicide Office to interview witnesses and take written statements. Patrol officers located the parents and brought them to the office. When working a new case, usually all available detectives pitch in to interview and take statements. The detective assigned the case generally interviews the suspect(s). After we discovered the mother had another child die of Sudden Infant Death Syndrome in the past, she quickly became the focus of the investigation. After interviewing the three ladies who were at the house, we were stumped. They all insisted the children were alive and well when the parents left on the bus. Victoria babysat them, as she often did.

The parents were still being interviewed, and everyone else had been interviewed, except Victoria. Protocol required that two detectives interview juveniles. Detective Holguin and I interviewed Victoria. We asked her what happened, and she started telling her story. Not five minutes into her account, when Victoria was looking at the floor, I looked at Jimmy. He nodded. We were both surprised. Her inconsistent account of the details, demeanor, and mannerisms betrayed the truth. She murdered the children. She gave a written statement but denied harming the children. Later she changed her story and confessed to both murders. Her confession was consistent with the physical evidence and the medical examiner's finding that the cause of death was asphyxiation. All the evidence pointed to Victoria. We didn't see it at first, because other suspects made more sense.

The trial was that fall, and it gained national attention. Not because two babies were murdered, but because the accused murderer was a twelve-year-old girl. Here's how the Associated Press reported the story,

> Victoria Dalton walked into court Tuesday, a day after turning 13, wearing her hair in a ponytail, sporting a dainty white sweater and rubbing her eyes like any sleepy child.
>
> Then she went on trial for murder.
>
> Prosecutors portrayed her as a streetwise little girl, fascinated by horror, who smothered a 2-year-old girl and a 5-month-old boy living with her.[2]

Nobody wanted to believe twelve-year-old Victoria murdered two children in her care. That scares us. That tells us something about humanity. That tells us something about ourselves. After the two-week trial, Victoria Dalton was convicted of murdering Timothy and Rene by suffocating them with a pillow.

~

Emotion-based faith normally works like this: we are told something, from what we consider to be a reliable source. What we're told sounds reasonable and we *want* it to be true, so we believe it is true. We believe it to be true without investigating the premises for the claims. Emotion-based faith is why grown people fall for scams. Somebody emails them with an official looking email and claims to have money to deposit into their account. It looks like a reliable source, it sounds reasonable, and they want it to be true, so they believe it is true. The victim provides their account number and password to some con artist on the other side of the world who drains their bank account. But emotion-based faith starts long before we are adults. Children believe in Santa Claus because somebody they trust (e.g. a parent) tells them Santa Claus is real and brings them presents (they find that good). They want him to be real, so they believe Santa Claus is real.

Many deeply held beliefs are established on emotion-based faith, including many religious beliefs. People are told something by a religious leader (someone they trust). What they are told is good (or bad if you don't do something required—like give money). Because it is something they want (i.e., healing, wealth, or heaven) or something they fear (i.e., death, poverty, or hell) they believe the message and do what they are told.

Emotion-based faith isn't necessarily blind faith. Quite often there is some truth mixed in to make the promise seem plausible. Take for example worldviews. There are a number of worldviews. One author categorizes them into five major views: naturalism (atheism, agnosticism, and existentialism), pantheism (eastern and new age religions), theism (Christianity, Islam, and Judaism), spiritism/polytheism (thousands of religions), and postmodernism.[3] They all can't be right. In fact, only one can. Of these five worldviews, only naturalism and theism claim to be founded on evidence-based faith. Pantheism purports that humans are spiritual beings and one with the "ultimate reality." The material world, with all its pain and evil, is simply an illusion. Spiritism and polytheism teach there are many spirits and/or gods. These spirits or gods are made known through a person with special access or communication with them. Postmodernism holds that truth is relative to one's culture.[4] Of the five views presented, most Americans are theists. If only two of the five worldviews claim to be founded on evidence-based faith, what drives others? Emotion does.

Evidence is often trumped by emotion. Children wake up Christmas morning and find presents under the tree. Where did they come from? They weren't there the night before. To them the obvious conclusion is Santa Claus brought them, hence Santa Claus is real. People fall for scams because con artists play on people's emotions, most often their greed or fear. When we allow our emotions to drive our beliefs and ultimately our decisions, we often make the wrong choices.

It's easy to see the faulty reasoning of a child's belief in Santa Claus or an adult falling for a scam. But it's not so easy detecting emotion-based faith in other areas. Sometimes when people question what doesn't make sense, they are told not to ask questions—just have faith. Have faith in what?

Faith must have an object. Faith must be in something or someone. And that something or someone must be trustworthy. When I fly on an airplane, I have faith in both the aircraft's integrity and the pilot's ability. Yet, some hold on to emotion-based faith even when presented with evidence that what they believe is not true. Why? Because of the possible ramifications of it not being true. If Santa Claus isn't real, the child won't get any presents—or so they believe. If one's religious belief is wrong, where does that leave them?

Emotion-based faith is easy to spot. People say things like, "I don't believe she murdered the children" or "I believe God exists." Neither statement by itself supports the premise believed. Whether a twelve-year-old murdered two children or whether God exists, does not depend on what a person believes—or doesn't believe. Believing something to be true doesn't make it true.

Law enforcement officers operate in the world of evidence-based faith. Remember Sergeant Joe Friday's famous tag line, "Just the facts, ma'am"? Faith and belief are inseparable. We put our faith in what we believe to be true. When I walk into a restaurant I've never been to before to eat a meal, I am showing a tremendous amount of faith. There are several things I believe to be true about the restaurant. Some things I believe are the restaurant sells food, has safe food available for purchase, and that I will be served. Why do I believe all these things are true? Because my faith is based on empirical evidence of past experiences with other restaurants. The empirical evidence is the object of my faith.

The object of our faith is important.

In the last chapter, we learned mechanical devices and individuals are not the best places to put our faith. Although we must trust in mechanical devices and people to live our lives, is there something solid, unchangeable, and always reliable that we can put our faith in that will give us the hope we long for? If we can't trust mechanical devices and individuals, how about societies, systems, or science? Let's quickly explore these.

Societies

At their core, societies are simply collections of people. Merriam-Webster defines society as "companionship or association with one's fellows" and "a voluntary association of individuals for common ends."[5] If individuals are inherently immoral, will a collection of them be moral?

Homicide detectives often discuss their cases with other detectives and/or their sergeants. It's a safe place to bounce ideas off others and get insight about how to best investigate. On May 21, 1994, Detective Dave Evans was slotted for the next case, and it wasn't long before we had another murder. Patrol officers on San

Antonio's Southside notified the Homicide Office they were on the scene of an apparent murder. Dave and Detective Joe Rios responded. A few hours later, they returned. The pictures were especially disturbing, even for a homicide detective. A teenage girl's nude body was found dumped like a piece of trash. She had been beaten, bitten, and impaled with a stick.

Dave's investigation revealed that sixteen-year-old Adria Sauceda got drunk at a party and was raped by several young men. She started to regain her senses in time to stop twenty-one-year-old Humberto Leal Jr. from raping her. Leal complied and even feigned sympathy. When she needed a ride home, Leal volunteered. That's the last time she was seen alive.

The evidence quickly pointed to Leal, even the bite marks on Sauceda matched his teeth impressions. Leal gave a signed confession, was convicted of capital murder, and sentenced to die by lethal injection. In 2011 he was executed.

More than twenty-five years after the murder, I contacted Dave.[6] He remembered the victim's name, the suspect's name, and all the details. Things stay with officers. Some things officers will carry with them their whole lives.

T he gang of thugs who raped Adria meets the definition of a society. Many people, especially Americans, believe in majority rule (although we are a representative democracy and constitutional republic, not a direct democracy). In a direct democracy, where the majority rules, the majority makes the rules. Hence, if the majority agrees to something, it is believed to be right—even moral. Ask the young lady who was gang raped if she agrees.

No, morality isn't the collective opinion of a majority of people, be they a microcosm or a macrocosm of humanity. Throughout history great societies have proven to be inhumane (e.g. the Assyrian Empire, Mongol Empire, and Nazi Germany). Nor is the opinion of those in authority necessarily moral. If individuals are inherently evil, a group of them isn't going to be inherently good. Does that mean all societies are evil? No, not all. Just like every human being is not as evil as they are capable of being, neither is every society. In fact, most are not. Most people do not live to kill or destroy others. But, as we have seen, everyone is capable of evil. Even twelve-year-old girls. Societies are made up of inherently immoral people and a group of them is not inherently moral.

Systems

Since individuals and societies can't be trusted to always be right, what about systems? When I first started with the SAPD, I got in the habit of following up on my arrest cases by contacting the follow-up unit or the district attorney's office. To my disappointment I found many of the cases were dismissed or plea-bargained down to a lesser offense. A wise veteran officer advised me not to worry about the final disposition of the case, just do my job and let the chips fall.

President Ronald Reagan famously said, "The most terrifying words in the English language are: 'I'm from the government and I'm here to help.'" As President of one of the greatest governmental systems in history, Reagan knew better than to trust a system created and run by human beings. As good as the American system of government is, it has flaws. Every system of government is flawed. One can find good and bad in all governmental systems, be they aristocracies (rule by the best), oligarchies (rule by the few), monarchies (rule by a sovereign), or democracies (rule by the people). Systems are necessary. Systems are good. Some systems are great. But systems, like people, are flawed.

Law enforcement officers are part of a system—the criminal justice system. The American system of criminal justice is a good one. A very good one. But it's not perfect. America's system is based on the due process model that seeks to protect the rights of the individual over the state. The accused is presumed innocent and the burden to prove guilt lies with the state. Defendants are afforded a number of rights and the state must prove its case based on proof beyond a reasonable doubt to an unbiased jury. The trial is held in open court presided over by an impartial judge. From the time government officials (i.e., law enforcement officers) begin their investigation into a crime, due process begins. Law enforcement officers, prosecutors, court officials, and anyone acting on their behalf are held to rules designed to protect the rights of the accused and provide justice. In a perfect world, it works just that way. But we don't live in a perfect world and mistakes are made, rules are broken, and injustice happens. From the LEO's perspective, criminals get away with crime because of a technicality, a simple mistake, or corruption within the system.

The potential for corruption is why American's founding fathers built checks and balances into our system of government. A system is no better than the sum of its parts, and when there's a broken part, the system fails. Officers rarely testify in court. Most cases are dismissed outright or plea-bargained and never go to trial. A plea-bargain is when the defendant agrees to plead guilty to a lesser charge. This is supposed to be a winning scenario for all involved. The defendant receives less punishment, the victim gets the satisfaction of a guilty verdict, and taxpayers are saved the cost of a trial. However, where's the justice? The little child in the LEO cries out "That's not fair!" and they become frustrated with the entire system.

Science

Angela Martin was found stabbed to death on the kitchen floor of her apartment. Her toddler son was found at the house, unharmed. There were no signs of forced entry. No property was missing. She was not sexually assaulted. The autopsy revealed Angela sustained more than twenty stab wounds, many of which were post-mortem. Over kill. Anger appeared to be the motive. In the months before her murder, Angela filed police reports against her ex-husband, Nathan Martin. After their divorce, Nathan stalked her. He habitually parked his truck outside of her workplace and watched. He was also seen watching her apartment. A man she dated had the brake line on his car mysteriously cut. Someone drilled a hole through Angela's apartment wall from inside a storage closet attached to her apartment. The hole made it easy for someone to spy on Angela. This was prior to Texas stalking laws, and Nathan couldn't be tied to the cut brake line or the hole in the wall. Everything pointed to Nathan, but I had no physical evidence that connected Nathan to the murder. Nothing except one fingerprint.

The crime scene unit lifted a fingerprint from a glass that was found on the kitchen table. It was Nathan's.

I brought Nathan in for questioning. He denied murdering his ex-wife and claimed he was with his teenage nephew the night of the murder. Nathan provided a written statement in which he swore under oath that he didn't kill Angela and wasn't at the apartment the night of the murder. In fact, he said he hadn't been there for some time. When confronted about the fingerprint, Nathan had nothing to say. That fingerprint was the piece of critical evidence that led to his conviction. Nathan Martin remains in the custody of the Texas Department of Corrections serving a life sentence.

Scientific evidence helped convict Nathan Martin of murder. But the fingerprint alone couldn't have done it. There were no witnesses, we didn't find Angela's blood on Nathan, and he didn't confess. The fingerprint had to be put in context. It was found at the scene of the crime, placing Nathan there. Angela made reports against Nathan. Nathan's child was not harmed. The crime appeared to be out of anger. When Nathan denied being at the apartment, he lied. Putting it all together, the state proved beyond a reasonable doubt that Nathan murdered Angela.

What about science? Surely, we can put our faith in science. Trust science, really? How often do meteorologists get the weather right? Scientists once told us the world was flat, the sun revolved around the earth, and the universe was static. During the 2020 COVID-19 pandemic, Americans were told over and over again to trust the science. At first, we were told not to wear masks because the science said that they don't work to stop the spread of the virus (although they mysteriously worked for medical personnel). Then we were told to wear masks, some states even required wearing masks because the science said they work to stop the spread. Does that mean the science was wrong?

Merriam-Webster defines science as "the state of knowing; knowledge as distinguished from ignorance or misunderstanding" or "a system or method reconciling practical ends with scientific laws."[7] Scientific laws do not change, that's why they are called laws. The presumptions, assumptions, suppositions, and theories are where troubles arise. At one time, scientists believed the sun revolved around the earth, because that's what it looks like from our perspective. But when Copernicus did the math, he discovered that the sun, not the earth, was the center of our solar system The universe didn't change after scientists discovered that planets revolve around the sun, our understanding of reality changed.

Science, when properly understood, accurately applied, and unbiasedly interpreted leads to the truth. The problem is that the data is interpreted through the lens of finite understanding, human error, and biases. The truth be told, scientists don't know everything, make mistakes, and misinterpret data.

∾

So, where are we left? What can we trust to be the object of our faith? Should we avoid trusting another person, societies, systems, or science? No, of course not. All of these can be trusted, and must be—to a point. However, we need to understand and accept that they all are flawed.

The question remains, *Is there something—or someone—that is absolutely moral, just, and reliable? Something—or someone—solid and unchangeable? All the time, every time?* If we can't place complete faith in each other, societies, systems, or science, what is left to be the object of our faith?

7

FAITH IN GOD

Now faith is the assurance of things hoped for, the conviction of things not seen.

—Hebrews 11:1

A twelve-year veteran police officer of a mid-sized American city and I were talking. He brought up the subject of religion and faith. Thoughtfully, he asked, "Isn't believing God exists mainly based on faith?"

My response was, "Yes, and believing God doesn't exist is also based on faith."

As we've established, we live our lives by faith, either emotion-based faith or evidence-based faith. The difference between the two is the object of our faith. Faith must have an object. We choose the objects of our faith, be it an alarm clock, a pilot, Santa Claus, or a religion. If an alarm clock proves itself unreliable, we lose faith in it and replace it. Some people fear flying because they don't trust the pilot's skill or the integrity of the aircraft. Some children believe in Santa Claus because mom and dad said he is real. Some adults follow a particular religious belief because they trust those who tell them it is true. Others believe because they have investigated the claims. The objects we choose to put our faith in are based on emotion or evidence. But as stated previously, believing something doesn't make it true.

Religious skeptics often say things like, "Prove to me God is true and I'll believe."

What do people mean by "proof"? Most people believe the earth is round, although they've never traveled around it or seen it from space. But there are pictures, and people that we trust (i.e., astronauts and scientists) who tell us the earth is a sphere. So, we believe—by faith. The objects of our faith are the pictures (that we trust are not altered) and people (we don't know) are telling us the truth.

Can we investigate evidence for the existence of God? [1]

Cops are skeptical. If they don't come to the job with a sense of skepticism, they soon develop one. Skepticism isn't a bad thing. In fact, a healthy sense of skepticism is necessary to be an effective officer. Rookie officers soon learn to doubt what people say and look for evidence to verify what they claim. Yes, LEOs are skeptical, but they're also rational.

Humans are rational creatures. Our ability to reason sets us apart from animals. Humans act with reason, and even against reason. We come to rational conclusions or say something is irrational. We consider possibilities and weigh them against probabilities. Therefore, we come to believe something to be true through reason. Believing something to be true is having faith that it is true.

Faith is defined as complete trust or confidence in someone or something. Faith is based on emotion or evidence. Emotion-based faith can get a person into trouble. Faith that something is true is best based on evidence that points to a reasonable conclusion. When evidence supports a crime was committed, and a suspect is responsible, an arrest is made. If a jury finds proof *beyond a reasonable doubt* that the accused is responsible, he or she is found guilty. So, I invite you to reason with me.

Most of the crimes LEOs deal with are over before they arrive on the scene. Hence, they must investigate to determine if a crime took place and the identity of a suspect. Officers use witness statements and look for evidence to determine what happened. A dose of healthy skepticism is in order. In fact, the staunchest skeptics often make the best detectives.

Assume the role of a detective and you've been dispatched to investigate a death. In a death investigation, the *cause* of death will determine if a crime has been committed but will not necessarily identify a suspect. There are four basic causes of death: natural, accidental, suicide, and homicide. When you arrive on scene, a patrol officer brings you a witness. The witness is a 16-year-old male who heard a single gunshot and saw a man wearing cowboy boots run from the area. Is the witness reliable? He lives in the area, has no ties to the victim, and appears to have no reason to lie. But his story needs to be compared to the physical evidence at the scene.

Here's our scene: The body is found inside a locked house, there are no signs of forced entry. The cause of death may be natural, accidental, suicide, or homicide. The victim is lying on the floor and has a single gunshot wound to the head. You quickly rule out a natural death. No gun or shell casings are found inside the house. Also, there is no evidence of a close contact wound. A single bullet hole is discovered in a window that faces the back yard that's surrounded by a wooden privacy fence. The broken glass indicates the bullet was fired from outside the house. It doesn't look like an accident or suicide. You have a homicide on your hands.

The scene expands to the back yard. You examine the fence and discover a hole was recently cut into the fence, just big enough to point a gun through. The hole lines up with the hole in the window. On the other side of the fence you find one spent 9mm shell casing, several Marlboro cigarette butts, and heel prints from men's cowboy boots. While not identifying a suspect, the evidence points to a chain-smoking, cowboy boot-wearing murderer, who shot his victim with a

9mm. From the evidence, that's a reasonable conclusion and it agrees with the testimony of the witness.

～

A much more difficult question is, "Does God exist?" And, if he does, is it possible to *know* that he exists? The God that Christians worship is a spirit. Jesus said, "God is spirit, and those who worship him must worship in spirit and truth."[2] A spirit can't be seen, nor touched. Hence, if God is a spirit, he can't be seen. He can't be touched. We can't taste God or smell him. People claim they hear from God, but is that just something in their minds? Unless God reveals himself to us in a way that we can grasp through our senses— apart from the testimony of the Bible—can we know God exists? Is there evidence we can examine? Yes, there is.

Let's take a quick look at the evidence and compare it to statements made in the Bible. Like the witness' statement at the death investigation, I'll not ask you to accept the Bible's witness as accurate without a proper examination of the evidence. The Bible begins by making a statement about the existence of God and the beginning of the universe, "In the beginning God created the heavens and the earth."[3]

The opening statement of the Bible is either true or false. There's no in between. Either God did create the heavens and the earth, or he did not. There's no other choice. Whether he created in six literal days, over the course of many years, by a process called evolution, the Gap theory, or any other means is not the question we're addressing here. Our question is simply, "Does God exist?" Since we cannot experience God with our five senses, like a detective, we must look at the evidence. The question, "Did God create the heavens and earth or not?" is basic to God's existence. If God does not exist, he did not create. But if God did create the heavens and the earth, then that itself proves his existence. Like a piece of art is evidence an artist exists, is the universe evidence a Creator exists?

I can make philosophical arguments that God exists, but many philosophical arguments get bogged down in muddy and controversial metaphysical issues that people disagree about.[4] I could argue that every person, everywhere, has a deep, inner sense that God exists, and that he is their Creator.[5] But rather than argue philosophically, we'll do what cops do—investigate.

We'll approach the question "Does God exist?" like a detective approaches a death investigation. The evidence needs to be examined, hypotheses made, conclusions drawn, and a case presented. We'll treat the world we live in as one large crime scene and try to answer the question, "Does God exist?" Let's take a look at the evidence. As we do so, we'll also look at Scripture to see if the testimony from the Bible aligns with the evidence.

The Evidence

A good investigator will examine the evidence and try to set aside any personal biases or preconceived notions. Relying on experience and expert witnesses, the detective will interpret the evidence to come up with the most *reasonable* explanation for the cause of death. We'll do the same, except we'll come up with the most reasonable explanation for the cause of life.

The crime scene before us is the world, nay, the universe, in which we live. What do we know about it? At least four things:

1. The earth is real, it exists. This begs the question, "Was there a time when it did not exist?" For a long time, many scientists believed the universe—the heavens and the earth—always existed. If this were true, Genesis 1:1 would be untrue. God cannot create something that already existed. In 1929, Edwin Hubble discovered that the universe is expanding. This became known as Hubble's law. Because galaxies are not static, the evidence demonstrates our universe had a beginning. In other words, there was a time when the heavens and earth did not exist.

2. The earth is complex. It has both macro and micro systems. One author writes, "The Earth system is a

complex functioning system that includes all the components of the various 'spheres.'" [6] These spheres include the *lithosphere* or the solid earth. The *atmosphere*, which is the gaseous envelope surrounding the earth. The *biosphere* that comprises all living organisms; and the *hydrosphere* or the water system.

3. Things have purpose. Taking a closer look at living organisms we find they are all made up of cells. We take the evidence to the lab to be scrutinized under a microscope and find that the simple single cell isn't as simple as first thought. Not only that, cells have purpose. They function within systems, highly complex systems.

4. Earth uniquely sustains life. We travel up to an observatory and look out into space only to find that there too are complex systems. We discover that if the earth were closer or farther from the sun, it could not sustain life. We also find the thickness of the earth's crust, the earth's relationship to the moon, and the earth's atmosphere are all favorable to life. [7]

By our brief observation of the "crime scene" this is what we know: Earth had a beginning, it is highly complex, things have purpose, and earth uniquely sustains life. Although, all this could be random, it appears someone is behind what we see. Israel's King David contemplated this and concluded God is behind it all, "I look at your heavens, the work of your fingers, the moon and the stars, which you have set in place." [8]

There's no disputing these simple facts. What we know from personal experience is that, setting aside the essence of God, for something to exist it must have had a cause. In our experience, nothing happens without a cause. For a row of dominos to fall over, the first one must be pushed. Scientists believe the universe came into existence with what they call the *Big Bang*. According to Space.com:

At its simplest... [the Big Bang Theory] says the universe as we know it started with a small singularity, then inflated...to the cosmos that we know today.... In the first second after the universe began, the surrounding temperature was about 10 billion degrees Fahrenheit (5.5 billion Celsius), according to NASA.[9]

But what or *who* caused the bang? Who pushed over the first domino? Strangely, this huge explosion produced an orderly solar system, fine-tuned to sustain life on the planet we call earth. For something to be orderly, there must be intentional design. Order doesn't just happen—*it must have purpose.* In fact, according to the second law of thermodynamics, everything, by nature, moves from order to disorder. The aftermath of any explosion I've seen is disorder, not order. For something to be orderly, there must be an intentional outside cause. What is the cause of our orderly and complex universe? Can it be explained through natural, physical causes and processes? Or, is there a *Being* behind the heavens and earth?

The evidence indicates that the heavens and earth have a cause, a design, and a purpose. It's almost as if someone put them in place. The Bible declares, "By the word of the Lord the heavens were made, and by the breath of his mouth all their host."[10]

But there's more. There are two other types of evidence: mental and moral.

1. Mental. Somehow nonmaterial consciousness emerged from unconscious matter. Humans make mental choices in an otherwise "cause and effect" universe.[11] A tree is struck by lightning, splits in two, dislodges a rock, that rolls down a hill—cause and effect. A person at the bottom of the hill sees the rock coming and decides to move—a mental decision.
2. Moral. Transcendent, objective moral truths exist.[12] For some reason, humans have an intrinsic sense of right and wrong. Why? Somehow, we know right from wrong. Anthropologists confirm that throughout all cultures there is a moral code inside every person. John Stott writes "to everybody everywhere...there is a difference

between right and wrong, and that evil deserves to be punished."[13]

How did an explosion of physical matter cause humans to have the ability to reason and decide? Even more, why do we have a sense of morality? When testifying before Felix, the Apostle Paul said, "I always take pains to have a clear conscience toward both God and man."[14]

But what does the evidence tell us about what or who started the Big Bang? What caused the bang? Is there a *Being* behind the Big Bang? If so, who is the most likely suspect? This is where possibility v. probability comes into play.

Possibility v. Probability

To make a legal arrest for a crime, the evidence against the accused must rise to the level of *probable cause*. In other words, an officer must demonstrate, by the evidence, that it is probable that the suspect committed the crime. To be convicted in criminal court, the prosecution must provide proof *beyond a reasonable doubt* that the accused committed the crime. What level of proof do we have that the universe came into existence by accident verses the intentional actions of an intelligent being?

No reasonable investigator would rule out the possibility of either being true. A reasonable investigator sets aside his or her biases and examines the evidence in light of possibility v. probability. A *possibility* means there's a chance, however so slight, that an event did or might occur. A *probability* means it is likely that an event did or will occur.

Take our death investigation. Remember, there are four basic causes of death: natural, accidental, suicide, and homicide. Is it possible the death was natural? There's a *possibility* that just before the bullet struck the victim, he had a brain aneurism and died of natural causes and the bullet simply struck a dead body—but is that *probable*? There's a possibility our victim shot himself and someone removed the gun, wiped away gunshot residue that indicated a close-contact wound, went outside, shot a hole through the window to make it look like murder, went back inside recovered the bullet he shot and repaired any damage to the wall, but is that *probable*? There's even a possibility that it was accidental. Perhaps the shooter was just standing on the other side of the fence, smoking cigarettes when his gun accidentally discharged, through the small hole in the fence and hit the victim in the head. It's possible, but is it *probable*? It's also possible that it was an intentional act—a murder.

Is it possible, that a cowboy boot-clad man waited, smoking cigarettes, with gun in hand, peered through the hole in the fence until the victim walked into sight? Is it possible that the man pointed the gun through the hole in the fence, aimed, and pulled the trigger? Is it possible the bullet went through the window and struck the victim in the head, killing him instantly? Is it possible the suspect fled, left behind footprints, a shell casing, and cigarette butts? Is it possible that a witness saw a man wearing cowboy boots flee just after hearing a gunshot? This scenario is not only *possible*, it's *probable*. While it's *possible* that the victim died from a natural cause, by accident, or suicide, the most *probable* explanation from the evidence is murder.

Death investigations take time. We all agree it's critical for investigators to do a thorough job, for fear of allowing a murderer to go free or an innocent person be convicted. But after all the evidence is collected and the case presented, the jury must act on faith. They must determine, based on the evidence presented, if the accused is guilty beyond a reasonable doubt.

Just as a homicide investigation points to the actions of someone causing the death of another, so too does an investigation of our universe point to the actions of someone causing the world and life itself. Who is the most likely suspect? It's a being we call God. The evidence points to the fact that God does exist.

My personal investigation led me to believe the God of the Bible is the God behind creation. For a more thorough investigation of God's existence and the veracity of the Bible see *Cold-Case Christianity* and *God's Crime Scene* by J. Warner Wallace.

I'm not asking you to take my word for it, I'm asking you to examine the evidence yourself. In the end, you will have to take a step of faith. Albeit, it's not blind faith. Just like a detective, you will have to consider the evidence before you and make a determination of possibilities v. probabilities. The Bible says, "By faith we understand that the universe was created by the word of God, so that what is seen was not made out of things that are visible."[15]

It's not a question of whether or not a person has faith. Everyone does. The questions are, "What kind of faith do you have, emotional-based faith or evidence-based faith?" and "What or who is the object of that faith?"

8

PAIN AND LOVE

Endure suffering.
—Saint Paul

P ain (or suffering) is the first woe in Frankl's triad of tragedy. Pain and suffering shouldn't be. They go against the way things must be in an ideal world. Hence, we regard pain and suffering as *evil*. Whether the pain and suffering of evil is self-induced, comes from natural causes, or is the result of another's devices, evil is not good and surely can't be part of a utopian society, one which we believe has the possibility of existing. It is that elusive, internal yearning for perfection.

So, what do we do with the pain and suffering we call evil? Some seek to escape pain and suffering at all costs. They try to medicate, avoid, deny evil exists, or end it by suicide. Some medicate with drugs (prescription or otherwise), alcohol, or other additions. Others seek to avoid pain and suffering by not allowing themselves to be vulnerable, be it physically or emotionally. The stoics tell us to grin and bear it with a stiff upper lip. Finally, some deny the reality of evil, and blame the actions of evil people on mental illness or some other biological, environmental, or psychological deficiency.

The fact is evil is real and law enforcement officers see it every day.

Homicide investigations are far reaching. In the 1990s, if a medical doctor didn't sign off on a cause of death, or the victim wasn't hospitalized for at least 24 hours prior to death, the SAPD Homicide Office started a preliminary investigation. Hence, as a homicide detective I was routinely called to deaths that occurred at residences. The worse were the infant deaths. Why would an apparent healthy infant suddenly die? As a detective, we were always suspicious and looked for any evidence the death was natural, accidental, or even murder. However, an unexplained death of an infant is not unusual. It's called Sudden Infant Death Syndrome or SIDS. The Mayo Clinic defines SIDS as

> [T]he unexplained death, usually during sleep, of a seemingly healthy baby less than a year old. SIDS is sometimes known as crib death because the infants often die in their cribs. Although the cause is unknown, it appears that SIDS might be associated with defects in the portion of an infant's brain that controls breathing and arousal from sleep.[1]

Natural or not, baby deaths were the most heartbreaking.

Early one morning in 1996, on the way to work at the police academy, I came upon a major accident that just occurred. It was a rollover on Loop 410 South, east of the IH 37 South interchange. The dust was still settling when I pulled over in my personal truck. The car came to rest upright, in a weeded area on the right shoulder of the highway. The rear window was missing and there was 80 yards of debris strewn out behind the car. Standing next to the car was a frantic young lady in her twenties. She was looking into the back seat and screaming, "Where's my baby? Where's my baby?" She saw me and started yelling the same question at me. The academy casual uniform of a polo shirt with the SAPD logo, a badge clipped on my belt, and my pistol instantly identified me as a police officer.

"Where was your baby?" I asked.

"In the back seat!" she screamed.

I looked in the back seat, it was empty.

"In a safety seat?"

"Yes, yes!"

"Okay, wait here. I'll go look."

I followed the trail of debris, plowed up dirt, and downed weeds back toward where the car left the highway. About 50 yards from the car I saw a child's safety seat, lying face down. I didn't know if the baby was in it or not. I rolled it over, and the child was there. He was dead.

People, even innocent children die by accident.

From 1987 to 1992, I was assigned to east patrol, in the 41 section, on Power Shift (5 p.m. to 3 a.m.). My district was 41-10. For much of that time, Officer Dave Moore worked the adjoining district, 41-20. Dave and I are about as different as night and day, but we worked well together and often covered each other. At 6'4", Dave was a good man to have on your side, and I was happy when we made calls together.

Halloween night, 1991, was cold, and extremely busy. An unusual call came in and Dave was dispatched. I was assigned as the cover officer.

The dispatcher called, "42-20."

"42-20," Dave replied.

"42-20, make ### Sherman for a disturbance, man chopped someone's head off."

"10-4, 42-20."

"41-10, cover."

"10-4, 41-10," I said and was on my way to back-up Dave.

Dave got back on the radio, "42-20, I'll let you know." Saying "I'll let you know," was informing the dispatcher to cancel the cover officer. It wasn't unusual to get prank calls, especially on Halloween, and this call had all the markings of a hoax.

I continued on, just in case, "41-10, I'm still en route."

"10-4, 41-10," the dispatcher said.

Another officer asked, if he heard the call correctly, "Did you say a someone's head was chopped off?"

"10-4, that's the report," the dispatcher advised.

Although tied up on other calls, sometimes officers can't resist smart-aleck comments. The sergeant generally let a couple comments go, as long as it didn't get out of hand. From time-to-time, most officers joined in on the fun, and I was no exception. It was a way to bring a little humor to a serious job. Officers use humor, often dark humor, to help insulate themselves from the evil they see on the job. This call was ripe for wisecracks.

Someone keyed his mic, "Look out for a guy named Jason!"

Another chimed in, "He might be wearing a hockey mask!"

I laughed to myself and continued to the call. I arrived just ahead of Dave. The street was dark, and it was difficult to find address numbers on the houses. I knew I was in the correct block and the house would be on the south side of the street. I slowly drove down the street looking for the house. I found it and parked my blue and white.

"41-10, 10-6 (at location)."

"10-4, 41-10," acknowledged dispatch.

While writing the manuscript, I contacted Dave and asked if he remembered the call. As I figured, he did. "Of course, I remember it. That was the strangest call. Came out as someone chopped someone's head off," he laughed. Here's how Dave recounted the call to me:

It was a bitterly cold night. I got the call and said I'd let dispatch know because I and everyone else thought it was a hoax. You beat me there—to cover me—and as I walked up the woman came to the door holding a towel to her face. I assumed you asked her what happened, and she pulled the towel away dropping her jaw. I saw all this as I was walking up to you. You turned to me with a look of total shock. I got on the radio and said, "Start everyone it's for real." The old man had fled to the back yard where there was a wooded ditch. You went towards the ditch and I circled the house. I found him hiding behind the house still holding the old long handled axe covered in blood.[2]

The victim had a large gash that opened up the entire left side of her face. The skin was sliced off and her jaw hung open revealing her jawbone and teeth, obviously unable to speak.

The attacker was a black male in his seventies. He lived with his wife and the victim, who was a prostitute. The three got into a fight over medication and he attacked her with an axe.

Try to convince a seasoned LEO humanity is basically good and evil doesn't exist. We haven't gotten any better over the past few decades. In fact, it has gotten worse.

Evil in America is growing. In recent years, evil is attested to on a regular basis by the murderers who routinely gun down students, parishioners, shoppers, and other innocents. Why do innocent babies die without explanation? Why do accidents take innocent lives? Why do humans savagely attack each other? Why is evil escalating in America? Is it drugs? There have always been drugs. Guns? There have always been guns in our country. Mental illness? There have always been mentally ill people living among us.

As America seeks answers to these questions and security measures are modified, new laws are implemented, killers are analyzed, and survivors are comforted, a theological question quietly haunts many: *Why does God allow evil?* Before we answer, we need to know somethings about God. The religions with the largest followers are Hinduism, Islam, and Christianity. Each has a different belief about God and the reason evil exists.

Hinduism began thousands of years ago in India. Brahman is the name for the god of Hinduism and is a divine spirit. Hindus believe that every person's spirit is part of the divine spirit and is not confined to the body and mind. Essentially, everyone is god, and their hope is that through a series of reincarnations (cycles of death and rebirths) their sins will be paid for through personal pain and suffering and that one day they can be free from the illusion of the physical. Hence, pain and suffering are punishment for sins committed in a past life. This is called karma. Hindus believe that the physical world (including our bodies and minds) is an illusion and therefore so is pain and suffering, although pain and suffering are truly experienced. The divine spirit (Brahman) is the only reality and the evil seen in the world is not reality. The way to see reality is by freeing one's self of all passions or desires through yoga meditation. Success will liberate a person from the cycle of death and rebirth.[3]

Islam was founded on the teachings of Muhammad who believed he was the last of the prophets that began with Adam and included Abraham. He believed he was commissioned to tell people that Allah is the one true god. People are to live lives that please him. Muslims believe everyone inherently knows right from wrong and people are given a free will. One day Allah will judge everyone for their choices. Hence, pain and suffering are the result of immoral choices people make. They believe Jesus was a prophet, albeit not God, and that Muhammad wrote the Koran, their scriptures.[4] The hope of Islam is that Allah will determine that a person's good deeds outweigh their sin.

While there are some similarities between Hinduism, Islam, and Christianity concerning the origin of evil, Christianity is different. Hinduism and Islam both teach pain and suffering are the result of humanity's bad choices, as does Christianity. However, the hope of both these religions rests with the individual's ability to find peace or do good. Christian hope is not in the individual, but in God. Let's briefly look at the God of the Bible and the question of evil.

Christianity follows the New Testament teachings of Jesus Christ, who affirmed the authenticity of the Old Testament scriptures. Christians believe that, in a general sense, creation reveals God. But specific details are given in the Bible. While creation reveals a God who knows, the Bible claims God is *all-knowing*. While creation reveals a powerful God, the Bible claims God is *all-powerful*. Christians also believe God is love. The Bible states plainly that "God is love."[5] Not that God possesses love, but that he is love. That means God is *all-loving*. Christian doctrine holds all that God is, he is fully.[6] There is never a time when God lacks in knowledge, power, or love.

If we accept that God is at the same time all-knowing, all-powerful, and all-loving, why does he allow evil to seemingly go unchecked? In our limited understanding we reason this way: if God is all-knowing, he *knew* it was coming. If God is all-powerful, he *could* have prevented it. If God is all-loving, he *would* have prevented it. So why didn't he? Is God also evil? Is he an immoral God? Or is our reasoning faulty?

First, we'll consider the philosophical answer, which is very short and direct. Just because we don't understand or believe a loving God can allow evil doesn't make it true. When we reason "a God of love would not allow evil" we have projected our limited knowledge and understanding of how God works onto the actions of an all-knowing God who understands all things. Essentially, we are creating a god that understands the world from our limited perspective—a god that we must understand. But that is not the God presented in the Bible. Here's what the Bible says about God, "God...does great things that we cannot comprehend."[7] The Apostle Paul writes, "For who knows a person's thoughts except the spirit of that person, which is in him? So also no one comprehends the thoughts of God except the Spirit of God."[8] Hence, the philosophical argument is silenced. But is that all, do we leave it there? No, LEOs examine the evidence available, so let's look at the evidence from scripture concerning God and evil.

The psalmist writes that "the Lord is good to all."[9] If that is true, how do we account for the atrocities in our country, and around the world—be they natural, accidental, or intentional? To the surprise of many, the Bible also says that God creates evil, "I form light and create darkness; I make well-being and create calamity; I am the

Lord, who does all these things."[10] Let's consider two words: *create* and *calamity*.

The Hebrew word translated *create* means to fashion or shape the conditions that cause something to happen.[11] It's the same word Moses used when he wrote, "God created the heavens and the earth." Next, the text says the Lord causes *calamity*. The word translated *calamity* in the English Standard Version is most often translated *evil* in other passages. Other translations translate it *disaster* or *bad times*. The clearest translation for this verse is from the King James Version, "I make peace and create evil."

The text states that God creates the conditions for evil to exist. How does that fit with a *good* God? Although we tend to focus on the second part of this verse, the first part explains the second. It reads, "I form light and create darkness." Darkness is created by the absence of light. Apply this reasoning to the second part of the verse, "I make peace and create evil." Evil is created by the absence of peace (*shalom*), it is God's peace or God himself. At Jesus' birth the angel announced, "Glory to God in the highest and on earth *peace*."[12] Why peace? Because he is Immanuel—God with us. Jesus is God the Son who came to earth and put on humanity. God became man yet retained his divinity. Evil is created by the absence of God—this is how God creates evil, just like darkness is created by the absence of light. Light isn't darkness, nor does light possess darkness. In the same way, God isn't evil, nor does he possess evil. Evil is the natural result of God's absence.

Why is there more darkness in our country than there was just a few years ago? It's simply a spiritual law: less light—more darkness, less God—more evil. Does that mean innocent victims are evil? No, it means when God goes, evil fills the void. We are becoming a godless society where everyone does what is right in their own eyes.

In the 1960s, in an attempt to remove God from schools, prayer and public Bible reading were banned from school. Less God—more evil, do you see a correlation? Since then there's been a push to remove God from the public square. The enemy's goal is to remove God from the heart. A 2015 study found that one in four unchurched adults are either atheists or agnostics. The study revealed that,

"Twenty years ago, 18 percent of skeptics were under 30 years old. Today that proportion has nearly doubled to 34 percent—nearly one-quarter of the total U.S. population."[13]

As Hinduism and Islam teach, so too does Christianity teach that pain, suffering, and evil are the natural result of human sin. But why do we yearn for a perfect society? Because eternity is in our hearts and with it, the imprinted idea of a perfect society, a civilization that existed before sin. Prior to Adam's disobedience in the Garden of Eden, all was right. Humanity had not been cursed by the triad of evil, guilt, and death. But sin changed everything. Sin is responsible for the triad of tragedy. So, why doesn't God put a stop to it? Can he? He can; and he will.

Above, we reasoned: if God is all-knowing, he knew it was coming. If God is all-powerful, he could have prevented it. If God is all-loving, he would have prevented it. God gave Adam a choice and he made it. We'll talk more about Adam's choice in another chapter. The question we want to address here is what, if anything, did God do about evil? We know that evil is the result of sin. Ultimately sin is disobedience to God, and a holy God cannot be in the presence of sin, just like darkness cannot be in the presence of light. Light always chases away darkness. Darkness has no power over light, nor does evil have power over God. Simply put, God and evil cannot exist together.

The Christian hope is that God promised to restore things to the way they were:

> And I heard a loud voice from the throne saying, "Behold, the dwelling place of God is with man. He will dwell with them, and they will be his people, and God himself will be with them as their God. He will wipe away every tear from their eyes, and death shall be no more, neither shall there be mourning, nor crying, nor pain anymore, for the former things have passed away."[14]

This restoration will follow the final judgment day. The question then becomes, who will experience this ideal world without pain and suffering? As mentioned earlier, the Christian hope is in God, not in the individual, an institution, or even a religion. God gives this life freely to those who will accept it. Here's the answer God gave to the Apostle John, "It is done! I am the Alpha and the Omega, the beginning and the end. To the thirsty *I will give from the spring of the water of life without payment.*"[15]

So why has God delayed judgment? Why hasn't God acted yet? What's keeping him? Pain and suffering are the result of sin. Delay in judgment is because of God's love. God is patient with humanity and his desire is for all to repent and reach out to him for salvation. "The Lord is not slow to fulfill his promise as some count slowness, but is patient toward you, not wishing that any should perish, but that all should reach repentance."[16] Why doesn't God want any to perish? Because God is love.

~

Understanding evil is one thing; doing something about it is another. Law enforcement officers and military warriors are in place to prevent, stop, and arrest evil. "To serve and protect" the public. Evil will never be completely eliminated by humanity; it will take an act of God—and he will act! But until that time what do we do with the pain and suffering? I don't mean on the job; I mean in our own lives. What do we do with evil? With the pain and suffering that comes into our lives and touches us personally? Frankl says since it can't be avoided, use it for good. He says to turn pain and suffering into "human achievement and accomplishment."[17]

Frankl's approach is not unlike that of Paul the Apostle who said, "suffering produces patience."[18] Using pain and suffering for good is far better than trying to medicate pain and suffering out of our lives. This doesn't mean refusing medical help to ease physical pain. It means not abusing drugs (legal or illegal) and/or alcohol in an attempt to mask or forget pain and suffering, be it physical or emotional. Frankl's approach is also better than avoiding pain and suffering by isolating from others—physically or emotionally. Some refuse to love in an effort to protect themselves from emotional harm. They might avoid heartbreak, but they'll miss the benefits of living.

Living is risky. Existing is much safer. But do you want to merely exist, or do you prefer to live? Achievement and accomplishment are best gained (and many times only gained) in relationships with others. Relationships are risky. Unless we're willing to risk being hurt, disappointed, or rejected we'll never achieve or accomplish our potential.

Although turning pain and suffering into achievement and accomplishment is better than a negative response, we must always keep in mind the hope that the God of the Bible offers that one day, pain and suffering will be gone. Paul the Apostle experienced pain and suffering unlike most people will ever experience, yet he wrote of his future hope, "For I consider that the sufferings of this present time are not worth comparing with the glory that is to be revealed to us." [19]

9

GUILT AND LOVE

*So often times it happens that we live our lives in chains and we never even
know we have the key.*
—Eagles "Already Gone"

I n 1987, the San Antonio Police Department (SAPD)
decentralized patrol operations by opening three new substations around the city. These substations were in addition to the
downtown central patrol, which continued operations out of headquarters, and the westside substation. This meant patrol reassign-
ments across the city. All officers were permitted to sign-up for the
shift and substation they wanted. The assignments were based on
seniority. With four years seniority, I was able to get the transfer I
wanted: east patrol on the Power Shift. The Power Shift was a ten-
hour overlap shift that worked from 5 p.m. to 3 a.m., four days a week.
Three days off each week, it didn't get much better than that! The
shift covered the hours when there were the most calls for police
service. Hence, we supplemented the 3-11 and Dogwatch shifts. Four
years wasn't a lot of seniority, and I ended up with Tues/Wed/Thurs

as my days off. But I didn't mind working weekends when things were hopping.

Officers with more seniority were able to get the highly sought-after weekend days off. Working only four day a week, and with different days off, I'd only see some officers on my shift once or twice a week. Such was the case with veteran Officer Tom Gray.[1] He was an African American officer, who was quiet and kept to himself. Tom was nearing twenty years on the SAPD and was a no-nonsense, old-school policeman. Tom wasn't a big man, but he was solid and tough as nails. Although we worked the same section, our districts were on opposite sides of the section and we rarely made calls together. When we did, he handled the calls quickly and didn't have patience for stupidity. In case you don't know, stupidity is a common human quality that assures job security for LEOs.

One weeknight, Tom jumped a burglar attempting to break into a house in the 100 block of South Mittman Street. The suspect fled on foot. Tom notified dispatch and gave chase, "41-40, I've got one running."

Like many LEOs, I loved a good chase. Although most prefer a vehicle pursuit, a foot chase will do to break up the boredom of a slow night. It was a slow night, and as you might imagine, several officers responded to assist.

The dispatcher replied to Tom, "10-4, 41-40. Location and description."

"He's running west from South Mittman. Black male, jeans, white shirt, 6', 200," Tom said.

Officers converged on the area from all directions and quickly had the suspect penned in a block. Officers closed in and the suspect wisely gave up. There were four or five officers standing around the suspect. Out-of-breath, and clearly aggravated, Tom approached the suspect to arrest him. The suspect saw that a black officer was going to make the arrest and played the "brother" card.

The suspect, looked at Tom and said, "Oh come on, brother." That was stupid.

"I ain't your brother," Tom said in a calm voice, then smacked the bigger man with an open hand that knocked him off his feet. That was "old school" policing. Before my time as a policeman, it was a no-no to run from the law. With that I went back in service. The suspect was not injured and was booked for burglary and evading arrest. Stupid wasn't against the law back then either.

Was it wrong for Tom to smack him? Yes. What Tom did was wrong. How about the rest of us who ignored the slap and went about our business? Were we wrong? Yes, we were. Street justice isn't justice, it's vengeance. Law enforcement officers are charged with enforcing the law, not carrying out punishment. Over my 24-year career on the SAPD, occasionally I saw officers use excessive force on prisoners. Compared to the number of physical arrests made, the abuse of force by officers was rare. Rare or not, it was (and is) wrong. So why do officers do it? Because LEOs, like everyone else, are human and prone to sin. Officers get frustrated with the criminal justice system that many times seems to let the bad guys get off with little or no punishment. The lack of accountability for their behavior emboldens criminals to disrespect authority even more. Still, LEOs are not justified in abusing their authority. They know better, and believe it or not, it bothers them. Why does it bother them? Because they swore an oath and their word means something. Officers swear to abide by the rules. When they break that oath, they feel guilty.

～

Guilt is the second woe in Frankl's triad of tragedy. Guilt causes us to have conflicting thoughts. On one hand we feel justified meting out street justice, on the other hand we know it's wrong. Guilt can be defined as "bearing responsibility for an offense or wrongdoing; [or the] remorseful awareness of having done something wrong."[2] Guilt may also be defined as "a cognitive and an emotional experience that occurs when a person believes that he or she has violated a moral standard and is responsible for that violation."[3] One psychologist believes that "a sense of guilt occurs when we violate our own inner code of conduct. Guilt is a message of disapproval from the conscience which says, in effect, 'You should be ashamed of yourself!'"[4] Without exception, everyone is guilty of violating acceptable standards of behavior. The standards we break may be family codes, school rules, work policies, or even criminal laws. Breaking the rules is called an *offense*. An offense is "something that outrages the moral or physical senses."[5]

When we break ethical or moral standards and hurt another, the relationship with that person is harmed and we experience guilt. An article on the *Psychology Today* website said what we fundamentally know to be true, "It's appropriate to feel guilty when you've done something wrong. Feeling the emotion of guilt for an action deserving of remorse is normal; to not feel guilty, in these cases, may be a sign of psychopathy."[6] A psychopath is someone who is entirely self-absorbed. It's a person with no regard for others and no remorse for their own actions. Their lack of both a conscience and a moral responsibility to other people is evident through antisocial behavior. Serial killer Ted Bundy is a prime example. A lack of remorse is an abnormal response to harming another person.

Conversely, it's normal to seek forgiveness and work to restore the relationship. We seek to ease guilt by making amends for our actions or justifying them. But why is feeling remorse or shame normal? Where does this emotion come from? Why do we feel guilty? We do so because we have a conscience, a moral compass, and we desire to maintain healthy relationships with others. We are inherently relational beings and we strive to maintain relationships, especially those that are most important. Not only that, we know that we must answer for our choices. Scripture says this about our moral compass, "their conscience also bears witness, and their conflicting thoughts accuse or even excuse them on that day when, according to my gospel, God judges the secrets of men by Christ Jesus."[7]

In *Winning a Gunfight*, I recount a homicide investigation in which, by all accounts, the suspect got away with murder. The victim was bludgeoned and stabbed to death. Although I had a suspect, and knew he was guilty, there was no physical evidence that linked him to the crime. A witness told me shortly after the murder she saw the suspect washing blood from a knife, and he admitted to her that he beat and stabbed the victim. But the witness was a relative of the suspect and refused to give a written statement or testify to what she told me in court. I interviewed the suspect and he denied any involvement. After following up on all the leads, interviewing several people, and reviewing physical evidence, I didn't have enough for the district attorney to accept the case for prosecution. The case was at a dead-end, it was heading for the PFI (pending further investigation) file. Then the suspect, on his own, came to the Homicide Office, looked me up, and confessed to the murder. After he signed the written confession, I asked him why. His answer was guilt. He had an overwhelming sense of shame and guilt for murdering another human being and his conscience drove him to confess it. For this man, his conscience could only be eased by confessing to the murder he committed. Guilt is a healthy emotion when it drives us to do the right thing.

But there's also an unhealthy guilt. This occurs when we are eaten up by shame or harm done to another over which we are not responsible. This feeling is called *false guilt* because it manifests many of the same feelings as healthy guilt, but the feelings are not derived from a true offense. They come from a lie that says we bear personal responsibility as an offender for: something we didn't do (e.g. we weren't there to stop the harm); something we unintentionally did (e.g. we harmed someone by accident); or something we were justified in doing (e.g. we shot someone who we believed was a threat). In America today, there is an aversion to harming anyone for any reason. This has led to police officers (and others who come to the aid of innocent victims) who use lethal force to suffer from false guilt.

False guilt can be brought on by a variety of situations. It's not uncommon for people to attempt "suicide by cop" in order to take their own life. "Suicide by cop" is intentionally presenting a deadly threat to a police officer to entice the officer to shoot. Another situation that brings false guilt to police officers is using deadly force against innocent persons. Law enforcement officers are trained to respond to a posed threat of any kind. When the stakes are high, unfortunate events can occur. For instance, our enemies in both combat and the war on terror understand our aversion to harming innocent people; hence, they use civilians as human shields, or to carry out bombings. Also, there are people who misrepresent themselves to LEOs using toy or nonlethal guns. This puts officers in precarious situations. Shooting an innocent person that appears to be a valid threat to the officer, fellow officers, or other innocents can lead to false guilt. Be careful to distinguish between false guilt and true guilt. In this book, we are addressing true guilt.

$\sim$

So, what do we do with guilt? We can't just ignore it and hope it will go away—it won't. Guilt must be dealt with to bring our lives back into balance and to be at peace with ourselves and others. Like pain, some seek to get rid of guilt at all costs. Attempts are made to medicate, suppress, or deny its existence. And, like pain, medication takes the form of drugs, alcohol, or other addictions to forget, or at least deaden one's shame or remorse. Others try to suppress guilt by doing good deeds, giving to charity, or doing some type of penitence to atone for their wrong behavior. Some try to quash guilt by justifying their actions. Law enforcement officers do the same. As mentioned above, it's often called street justice because LEOs lose faith in the criminal justice system, so they decide to right the wrong themselves. But it doesn't right a wrong, it creates a second wrong, an offense that adds to the burden of guilt. But guilt is more than a burden we carry; it's a bondage that restrains us.

Guilt is a debt owed to another. It is a captivity with only two ways out—payment or forgiveness. Sometimes we can pay the debt and make things right. But more often than not, we cannot make restoration for the hurt we caused and must be forgiven for things to be made right. Here's a simple example. Say you backed your vehicle into my truck and damaged it, you would be in my debt. You would owe me for the damages and would morally (and perhaps legally) be responsible to pay for the repairs. Or, I could forgive the debt and pay for the repairs myself. Either way, payment must be made to restore the truck. Either the *offender* (you) pays or the *offended* (me) pays.

For the vast majority of our personal relationships, there's only one remedy for guilt—forgiveness. Forgiveness is about relationships. Whether we're seeking forgiveness or giving it, there's something we need to know about it. Forgiveness is the tonic that restores relationships and frees both the offender and the offended from the bondage of guilt. Here's the paradox of forgiveness: *Forgiveness has a price, but it can't be bought.* Forgiveness must be freely offered and freely received. When forgiveness is offered, the offended person incurs the debt. When forgiveness is received, the offender is relieved of payment.

"But that's not fair!" we exclaim. True, forgiveness is not fair. Justice demands the offender pay the debt owed. However, mercy allows forgiveness. Either way the debt is paid.

Here's another paradox of forgiveness: *Refusing to forgive also puts the offended in bondage.* That's another reason God commanded that we forgive one another. The Bible doesn't say forgiving another is a good idea, highly recommended, or even strongly suggested. Forgiveness is commanded, "if one has a complaint against another, forgiving each other; as the Lord has forgiven you, so *you must also forgive.*"[8] In the Lord's Prayer, Jesus says that we are to pray, "Forgive us our debts, as we also have forgiven our debtors."[9]

True forgiveness is just that—it's forgiving the debt. It's wiping the slate clean. It's stamping "paid in full" over the offense. It's letting go. It is not holding the wrongful behavior over the offender for control or emotional punishment. "But that's so hard!" "You don't understand what he/she did!" Yes, forgiveness is hard; if it was easy, we probably wouldn't have to be ordered to do it.

Here are some important things to remember about forgiveness:

- Forgiveness doesn't mean forgetting.
- Forgiveness doesn't mean trusting.
- Forgiveness doesn't mean excusing behavior.

There are some things that we'll never forget, offenses against us so deep we'll take them to our grave. Memory, while at times seems like a curse, it is a blessing. Even the memory of bad things done to us is a blessing. Memory helps prevent future harm. It can help avoid unnecessarily putting ourselves in a vulnerable spot. Memory helps us relate to others. When we remember how bad we were hurt, it helps us treat others better.

Forgiving and trusting are separate issues. Nowhere does God command us to trust others, only him. In fact, the psalmist says, "It is better to take refuge in the Lord than to trust in man."[10] Forgiveness is given, trust is earned. You can forgive someone and yet, not trust them. Let me explain using my truck again (do you get the idea I like my truck?). Say you asked to borrow my truck. You later return it and apologize for backing into a tree and denting the bumper. I forgive you and incur the loss. The following week you again ask to borrow my truck. Hesitantly, I agree. Once again, you return it with damage caused by your poor driving and ask for forgiveness. Again, I grant forgiveness and incur the loss. The following week, you again ask to borrow my truck. I say no. Why? Is it because I haven't forgiven you? No, it's because I don't trust you to drive my truck! Trust is earned. In order for me to trust you driving my truck, I must see that you've learned the skills to drive it.

Does this mean we never trust anyone? No. We must trust other people. Relationships are built on trust. Without trust society cannot survive. Trust comes naturally. Children are taught *not* to trust strangers. That doesn't mean all strangers cannot be trusted. In fact, most can, but we're not willing to take that risk with our children. When we learn someone can't be trusted, we shouldn't put our faith in them until they regain our trust by proving themselves trustworthy. We all have intuition that helps us make the decision whether or not to trust someone. Intuition comes from listening to wise counsel, living life, and being in relationships with others. The longer we live and the more life experiences we have, the better our intuition becomes.

Forgiving doesn't mean excusing, downplaying, or making light of the offense. Nor does it mean the offender wasn't guilty of wrong behavior. Forgiveness is serious. Forgiveness isn't to be taken lightly, nor is it to be given flippantly. When forgiven by another, we should graciously receive the forgiveness and strive not to offend again.

～

W hat about God's forgiveness? There's a New Testament story that illustrates God's forgiveness. Jesus was in Capernaum teaching when four men wanted to take their crippled friend to him for healing. Jesus was in a house teaching and the men were unable to get inside to see him. Undaunted, they hauled their friend onto the roof, made a hole in the roof, and lowered him into the house. Jesus' response shocked the religious leaders who were in the room, "And when Jesus saw their faith, he said to the paralytic, 'Son, your sins are forgiven.'"[11]

"Your sins are forgiven!" Why did Jesus say that? The man came for physical healing and Jesus forgave him of his sins. He came seeking relief from physical suffering and Jesus gave him eternal life by forgiving his sin. Still the question, why? Why did Jesus do this? He did it because that's what the man needed. That's what everyone needs. We all need forgiveness of our sins. Remember, forgiveness has a price. Either the offender pays the price or the one offended pays the price. How can Jesus forgive the man his sins? Because of who Jesus is. The religious leaders understood the statement Jesus was making by saying, "Your sins are forgiven." Here's their response, "Now some of the scribes were sitting there, questioning in their hearts, 'Why does this man speak like that? He is blaspheming! Who can forgive sins but God alone?'"[12]

The religious leaders understood that all sin is ultimately an offense against God, and while we can forgive others of offenses against us, only God can completely forgive a person of sin. It was clear to the religious leaders that Jesus claimed authority that belongs exclusively to God. So how did Jesus have that authority? Simple, he is God. He is either God or claimed to be God and wasn't. There are no two ways about it. Hence, he was either God or a fraud. There's no saying he was a moral teacher, but not God. A moral teacher doesn't claim to be who he's not—especially God. What did the paralytic do to be forgiven? He received forgiveness by faith. Forgiveness must be freely given and freely received.

So, who pays? Remember, an offense incurs a debt. The debt of sin is death, "For the wages of sin is death."[13] But if the debt needs to be paid, and the payment for sin is death, who made the payment? Jesus did. That's why he, God the Son, became a man. He came to die for sin. As a man Jesus represented humanity, just as Adam did when he sinned. But Jesus never sinned. He kept God's moral and ceremonial laws perfectly and went to the cross to die in our place. At the Last Supper, Jesus said that the wine represented his death, "this is my blood of the covenant, which is poured out for many for the forgiveness of sins."[14]

Whether we're guilty of serious moral failure, abusing our authority, or fudging on overtime, we're all offenders and need forgiveness. And, we've all been offended by others and need to give forgiveness.

Forgiveness brings freedom.

10

DEATH AND LOVE

Thou know'st 'tis common; all that lives must die,
Passing through nature to eternity.
—Shakespeare (Hamlet)

To my best recollection, cadet class 83B started out with about 45 cadets, 33 of us graduated. Within six months of graduation, three officers quit. They spent more time in the academy than they did on the streets. Policing isn't for everyone. When the reality of what law enforcement officers see, face, and do hits home, some quit. Patricia Calderon was one of the 33 who stayed with it. Pat was a San Antonio girl who grew up on the city's Southside, and really enjoyed policing her hometown. She also enjoyed jewelry! For a short time in the late 1980s, I sold gold jewelry for a little extra cash. Not long before Christmas 1988, Pat sent me a message on the MDT, the Mobile Digital Terminal—the early computers put in our police cruisers. Pat asked if I still sold gold necklaces; I responded that I did. "Great!" she replied and said she'd contact me some time to buy one. She never did.

In the early morning hours of December 27th, 1988, two thieves stole cigarettes from a convenient store on San Antonio's northeast side. The store clerk called in the theft and gave a description of the suspects' vehicle. Just before 2 a.m., Pat spotted the suspect vehicle southbound on IH 35 and called for back-up. The suspects were stopped in my district, on IH 10 East near East Houston Street. I was tied up booking a prisoner and didn't respond to the initial call for cover. The officers who did respond found the stolen cigarettes in the car. The passenger, Luis Miller Jr., fled on foot, and Pat gave chase. Miller ran through the Point East apartments and into an area dense with brush that surrounded Salado Creek. At 2:15 a.m., Pat radioed, "He's taking off his jacket." Other officers in the area heard a splash and Pat scream for help—then only silence. Four hours later a dive team recovered her body from the creek. Miller was later arrested and charged with theft and evading arrest, both misdemeanors. Investigators never established how Pat ended up in Salado Creek. She was 26-years old and was survived by a husband and infant son.

Death is the final woe in Frankl's triad of tragedy. Philosopher Luc Ferry wrote this about death in his best seller, *A Brief History of Thought,* "[D]eath has many different faces. And it is this which torments man: for only man is aware that his days are numbered, that the inevitable is not an illusion...."[1] Death is an appointment we all have, and all will keep. The Bible says, "it is appointed for man to die once."[2] Death, like suffering and guilt will be experienced by everyone. Rock star Bob Dylan is credited with saying, "If you're not busy being born, you're busy dying."[3] Death is simply a part of life and we've come to accept it. Other than what we consider premature death, few of us question death. At least not out loud. Children do. Children often ask the hardest questions because they don't understand, and they don't pretend to understand. So, they ask questions like, "Why do people die?" Our glib answers might be, "That's just the way things are;" or "Grandma went to heaven to be with grandpa;" or "God wanted daddy to be with him."

Although, we might not question why, and we understand the science that all things, including our physical bodies, are breaking down and will not last forever, we sense that death just isn't right. We believe that's not the way things are supposed to be. And you're right. That's not how things started out. God created Adam and Eve to live forever, but something changed that. It's called the *law of sin and death*.

When God created the universe, he put in place physical laws. Without these laws the universe would spin out of control and fly apart. Scientists have discovered these laws and named them. Sir Isaac Newton is credited with discovering and/or explaining several laws, such as Newton's three laws of thermodynamics and his three laws of motion. Perhaps you recall something about Newton's laws of motion from science class: A body in motion will remain in motion, a body at rest will remain at rest. To every action there is an equal and opposite reaction. But Newton is best known for explaining the law of gravity. The law of universal gravitation states that every particle is attracted to every other particle in proportion to their mass and distance to each other. That's why objects fall to the earth. The earth is a huge mass and all the objects on the earth are attracted to it. Hence, objects fall to earth.

Laws are different from theories. Theories are educated guesses based on observation. Laws are fixed and unchanging. Laws never change, unless a supernatural force acts to interfere—these are called miracles. When God created, he not only put physical laws in place, he also put spiritual laws in place. One basic spiritual law—that's as basic as the physical law of gravity—is the law of *sin and death*. To understand the law of sin and death, we need to go back to the beginning.

After creation was finished, God put Adam and Eve in the Garden of Eden. Everything was as it should be—perfect. There was no sin. There was no death. God gave everything to the new couple. They were given free reign over the earth, dominion over the animals, and were permitted to enjoy all things. There was only one restriction. They were forbidden to eat of one tree that was in the middle of the garden. If they did, they would die. So, why did God even put the tree with the forbidden fruit in the garden? To give them a choice. God loved his creation, especially Adam and Eve, and he wanted them to love him in return. Love is a choice. Love can't be bought or coerced. Love is a decision. God gave them a choice, a choice to love or not to love. Foundational to love is trust. God provided everything for Adam and Eve to live happily ever after. But did they trust God? Did they love God? Was their faith in God?

You can't put your faith in someone you can't trust. Satan's first words recorded in the Bible were designed for mankind to doubt God's word. Satan said to Eve, "Did God actually say, 'You shall not eat of any tree in the garden'?"[4] The implication was that God was withholding something good. He was withholding pleasure, power, or something else he didn't want them to enjoy. It was a temptation for something more. What more could they have, except to be gods themselves? And that was Satan's temptation, "You will not surely die. For God knows that when you eat of it your eyes will be opened, and you will be like God, knowing good and evil."[5] By eating the forbidden fruit, they would know good and evil by experience. It's not that they didn't understand disobedience; it's that they never experienced the consequences of disobeying God—death. Disobey and they would know. And disobey they did.

The short-lived period of innocence ended in one brief moment of disobedience. Communion with God turned into hiding from God. Their disobedience caused immediate spiritual death—separation from God. They were unable to commune with God as they had before sin. Before their disobedience, Adam and Eve were "naked and were not ashamed."[6] Afterward "they knew that they were naked"[7] and were ashamed. In an effort to hide their shame and cover their guilt they sewed fig leaves as coverings. Their sin also resulted in physical death. Although not immediate, they began to die physically, "...you are dust, and to dust you shall return."[8] Hence, humanity became subject to the law of sin and death.

This spiritual law is just as real as the physical laws of nature. Just like the law of gravity cannot be escaped, neither can the law of sin and death. With the law of gravity, the smaller mass is always attracted to the larger mass. With the law of sin and death, sin always results in death.

Does this mean physical death is always a direct result of one's own sin? No. There are four basic causes of death: natural, accidental, homicide (justifiable and non-justified), and suicide. Natural death is the consequence of a fallen world that was cursed because of Adam's original sin. Adam's sin knocked over the first domino and they continue to fall. Accidental death is the result of imperfect humans who are marred by sin. We make mistakes because we're imperfect and people die. Murder is a sin committed by the offender that results in the unjustified death of an innocent person. Suicide is taking one's own life and is a direct result of one's own action.

Things didn't turn out like Satan promised. Satan said they would be "like God, knowing good and evil." In one aspect, it was true; they would know good and evil. "Then the Lord God said, 'Behold, the man has become like one of us in knowing good and evil.'"[9] On the other hand they would not be like God. Until they sinned, Adam and Eve had only experienced God's goodness and the blessing that comes from obedience to him. Disobedience brought a knowledge of sin they wanted no part of, death. "Sin when it is fully grown brings forth death."[10] The end result of sin is death— "the wages of sin is death."[11]

After they sinned, Adam and Eve tried to cover their tracks. They experienced something new: shame and guilt. They tried to cover their shame and guilt with fig leaves. But fig leaves didn't do, and God provided them clothing. He made them garments out of the skin of an animal. By God's grace, he provided a covering for their shame and guilt. But at what cost? Death. An animal had to die for them to be covered. "But that's not fair!" we complain, "The animal didn't do anything wrong." That's true, but Adam's sin affected the whole of creation. It's the law of sin and death.

What does the law of sin and death have to do with suicide? If the end of life is only death, there is no hope. If the triad of tragedy is all that life promises, then life is hopeless. Some believe that's all there is, and it's no wonder many live with a daunting sense of hopelessness hanging over their life like a dark cloud. This sense of hopelessness is not new.

An inscription was found in the ancient city of Thessalonica which read: "After death, no reviving, after the grave, no meeting again." One scholar writes about the message that welcomed visitors to a city that lacked hope, "A typical inscription on a grave demonstrates this fact. 'I was not, I became, I am not, I care not.' While some of the philosophers, such as Socrates, sought to prove happiness after death, the pagan world had no word of assurance."[12] But death isn't the end. There is hope.

There is a word of assurance, a word of hope from the Bible. The Apostle Paul wrote to believers in ancient Thessalonica, "But we do not want you to be uninformed, brothers, about those who are asleep [those who have died], that you may not grieve as others do who have no hope."[13] What hope? What about the law of sin and death? Humanity sinned and humanity must pay sin's debt—death. Simply put, death is separation. Physical death is the soul/spirit being separated from the body. The Bible teaches that when the soul departs from the body, death occurs.[14] Whether the soul departs and the body dies, or the body dies, and the soul departs is a question for medical doctors and theologians to answer. Whatever the case may be, at death the soul is separated from the body.

Spiritual death is the soul/spirit being separated from God for all eternity. That's the final punishment for sin, eternal death from the presence of God. Sin brought death, but can that be corrected? Can humanity be reconciled to God? God is just and his justice demands the law of sin and death be followed. If God allowed sin to go unpunished, he would not be just. But God also loves humanity and desires that all be made right, like it was in the Garden of Eden. The only way both God's justice and love can be satisfied is by sin's debt being paid and sinners being forgiven. That is why God the Son became man in the Person of Jesus Christ. And that is why Jesus had to die. The crucifixion is God's answer to sin.

Just as Adam represented all mankind and sin was passed down through the man, so too Jesus represented all mankind when he lived a sinless life and died as punishment for our sin. He didn't die for his own sin, he had none. The Bible says it this way, "For our sake he [God the Father] made him [Jesus] to be sin who knew no sin, so that in him we might become the righteousness of God."[15] Think of that. Jesus became sin for us so we can *become the righteousness of God*. That's love. "For God so loved the world, that he gave his only Son, that whoever believes in him should not perish but have eternal life."[16]

The sacrificial death of innocent animals to cover Adam and Eve's shame and guilt foreshadowed the death of Christ as the final and sufficient covering for sin. Did the crucifixion take God by surprise? No, that's why Jesus was sent. "The Son of Man came not to be served but to serve, and to give his life as a ransom for many."[17] God not only knew it was coming—he planned it. God didn't stop it—he ordained it. His love didn't prevent it—it caused it. The scripture records, "God shows his love for us in that while we were still sinners, Christ died for us."[18]

Jesus' died to free us from the law of sin and death, "For the law of the Spirit of life has set you free in Christ Jesus from the law of sin and death."[19] Hence, God's justice and love were both satisfied. But, as with Adam and Eve, God will not force his love and salvation on humanity. Salvation must be received through faith, by grace, in Jesus Christ. As mentioned earlier in the book, faith must have an object. The object of faith for salvation is God. He alone gives life eternal. The life he gives is through faith alone. That means it is by grace alone. One cannot work, buy, or inherit salvation. It is a free grace-gift of God. This gift is in Jesus Christ. It is his death on the cross that paid the debt of sin we owe. "For the wages of sin is death, but the free gift of God is eternal life through Jesus Christ our Lord."[20]

Things will return to the way God intended. Salvation freely given in Jesus Christ is the hope given to all who believe. Remember, the Apostle Paul's words to the believers in Thessalonica whose city's fathers proudly posted, "After death, no reviving, after the grave, no meeting again"? The apostle wrote, "But we do not want you to be uninformed, brothers, about those who are asleep, that you may not grieve as others do who have no hope."[21] Who are those who have hope? Paul continued, "For since we believe that Jesus died and rose again, even so, through Jesus, God will bring with him those who have fallen asleep."

Like Officer Patricia Calderon, we all have an appointment with death. It's the final woe of Frankl's triad of tragedy, but in Christ death is conquered.

11

PARADISE RESTORED

Without love, where would you be now?
—Doobie Brothers, "Long Train Runnin'"

So, what is the answer to Viktor Frankl's triad of tragedy, the triad of pain, guilt, and death? Hope. Hope is important. Hope gives life meaning. Hope gives us a purpose. Hope gives us a reason to go on. Hope is that inner, elusive yearning that is common to all humanity. A hope for more. A hope for new. A hope for better. It is a spiritual thirst that can only be quenched by God. We are more than a physical body and a mind capable of reason. We have a spirit that is not content with more, new, and better. More isn't enough, we yearn for *forever*.[1] New isn't the answer, it's *all things new*.[2] Better doesn't cut it, the spirit longs for *perfection*, a hope for perfection that can only be found in God. A belief in God that doesn't go against reason but is consistent with reason and the evidence of God we see in the world and find in our hearts. It's a faith that things will be made right and humanity will be restored to commune forever with the God of creation.

The loss of hope is why most warriors choose to end their own lives. Because they put their hope in *the things of man* (i.e., individuals, societies, systems, or science), they are left wanting. As we have seen, and most of us have experienced, putting our hope in the things of man is a recipe for disaster. Humanity, even with the best of intentions, will let us down. Although everything humanity does, whether it's the formation of societies, the creation of systems, or the interpretation of science may produce good, it is flawed. Hope needs to be in God.

To help warriors not to take the suicide option, we need to give them back what they lost or may be in danger of losing: *hope.* Warriors begin their careers as some of the most hopeful and optimistic people. Warriors restore things. That's what they do. They see a wrong and they make it right. They see pain and suffering and they fix it. Even in the face of danger, warriors take action.

Whiting Sweeting fled on foot into the cold January night to escape the law. With arrest warrant in hand, Constable Darius Quimby pursued. The warrant was for trespass, a minor property crime, yet Sweeting vowed not to be taken alive. He ran into the snow-covered woods, jumped on a large rock, and threatened to kill the first man who touched him. Undaunted by the threats, Constable Quimby came up behind Sweeting and pulled him from the rock to take him into custody. The two men engaged in a brutal fight. Sweeting overpowered the officer and struck him down with a fatal blow. That was January 3, 1791. The New York constable was the first American law enforcement officer killed in the line of duty. Yet, 229 years and over 25,000 line-of-duty deaths later, American LEOs are still on the job, risking their lives to protect ours.

When faced with interpersonal human aggression, 98% of people will have a phobic scale response; most submit and do nothing. Others run. But warriors stay and fight. In fact, warriors welcome the fight. A warrior looks for evil and seeks to rein it in. Facing danger is what warriors do. God puts something exceptional in the heart of a warrior. The Bible records that God said of Israel's greatest warrior, "I have found in David the son of Jesse a man after my heart, who will do all my will."[3] In the heart of every warrior is a God-given tenacity, a resolve, a determination to face evil and take action. Warriors were necessary to sustain Israel and warriors are necessary to sustain America.

Former army ranger and West Point professor, Lt. Col. Dave Grossman said, "The only thing that is holding our society together is the warrior.... Were we to go one generation without warriors, our society would cease to exist."[4] Read the account of a modern-day American warrior who walked into danger's face:

> "I gotta go handle a call, I love you; I'll talk to you later." The 54-year-old Ventura County Sheriff's sergeant didn't tell his wife the nature of the call on the evening of November 7th, 2018. It was for shots fired at the Borderline Bar & Grill in Thousand Oaks, CA. Three minutes after saying goodbye to his wife, Sergeant Ron Helus and a California Highway Patrol (CHP) officer arrived at the bar full of college students. The sergeant radioed dispatch, "One subject advised she didn't see him [the gunman] come out. We're making entry." The officers entered through the front door. Sergeant Helus made a second transmission, "We got multiple people down. We need a lot of ambulances." Gunfire suddenly erupted in the bar, Sergeant Helus was hit several times and went down. The CHP officer dragged the wounded sergeant out of the line-of-fire. Rather than facing any more officers, the assailant killed himself. Sergeant Helus died from his injuries.[5]

What drives officers to go where most are unwilling to go? Courage. Where does courage come from? Genetics? No; courage doesn't always run in families. Education? No; there are plenty of educated cowards. Money? No; money can buy foolishness, but not courage.

The word courage comes from the Latin word (cor) for heart. Webster defines courage as the "mental or moral strength to resist opposition, danger, or hardship."[6] Scripture tells us to be courageous, The Lord said, "Be strong and courageous."[7] Hence, courage comes from within—it's a decision. It's a resolve from inside. *Courage is a choice.* Courage comes from being on the side of right. King Solomon wrote, "The wicked flee when no one pursues, but the righteous are bold as a lion."[8]

~

When lawfully carrying out their duties, law enforcement officers are on the side of right. They face danger because it's the right thing to do. They swore an oath, and their words mean something. They promised to protect, and that's what they do—no matter the cost. When danger threatens, the police are summoned and take action—warriors are necessary. They do things most wouldn't dare do. Warriors are different.

Different makes us uncomfortable. Warriors come in all shapes and sizes. Some are loud and outgoing. Some are quiet and reserved. They come from all walks of life, from every ethnic group, background, and social class. But unlike most people, warriors are kept at arm's length. They are hard to understand. Some say they are arrogant, egotistical, pigheaded, or overconfident. Some are. Perhaps this comes from their warrior's heart. God gives each of us a heart and a personality to do what he has called us to do. No matter the personality he gives, we can take it to the extreme.

Although different in some ways, there's something that warriors have in common with everyone else—they need to be forgiven.

The Bible is clear, the taking of human life in justifiable war, in defense of the innocent, or in self-defense is not forbidden by God. In fact, we are told that duly appointed soldiers and law enforcement officers are God's ministers and they "do not bear the sword in vain."[9] But, are there warriors who act outside the law? Yes, some do. Are there warriors who overreact? Yes, many do. Are there warriors who sin? Yes, all do.

We hear complaints about officers using excessive force, driving too fast, living immoral lifestyles, or simply being rude. And because they are authority figures and wield power over us, we tend to hold everything they do against them. Should officers be held to account for wrong behavior? Absolutely. Every agency has an internal investigative division and/or policy. The FBI has a special unit specifically dedicated to investigating complaints against law enforcement officers.

But remember this, officers come from our society. When we have a perfect pool of applicants to draw from, we'll have perfect officers—but then again, in a perfect society law enforcement wouldn't be needed. So how about extending a little grace and forgiveness? After all, we pray, "forgive us our debts, as we also have forgiven our debtors."[10] That comes from what we call *The Lord's Prayer*. What is the *Warrior's Prayer*? It is found in Psalm 51, a psalm written by King David. Warriors know, better than anyone else, they need forgiveness. Hear the words of Israel's greatest warrior, "For I know my transgressions, and my sin is ever before me."[11] So, what is the *Warrior's Prayer*? Look, "Have mercy on me, O God, according to your steadfast love; according to your abundant mercy blot out my transgressions. Wash me thoroughly from my iniquity, and cleanse me from my sin!"[12]

The only hope a warrior has is the only hope we all have—to be forgiven by God.

Sometimes warriors can't restore things. Sometimes warriors can't make things right. Sometimes they can't fix the pain and suffering. Then what? There's a story in the Bible about a warrior who had things figured out. This man was a Roman centurion. A centurion was a Roman officer in charge of 100 soldiers. In the first century AD, Roman soldiers were stationed throughout the empire to ensure the *Pax Romana*—the peace of Rome. So, I suppose we can say they were early peace officers. These soldiers were a tough lot. Most were war veterans. They knew how to keep the peace and did so.

In Jesus' day, a servant of the centurion stationed at Capernaum fell sick and was near death. Local Jews respected the centurion. Hearing Jesus was in town, the centurion sent Jewish leaders to ask him to heal the servant. The Jews pleaded with Jesus, "[The centurion] is worthy to have you do this for him, for he loves our nation, and he is the one who built us our synagogue."[13] This Roman warrior was not only a worthy soldier, he was a powerful administrator, a political leader, and a commendable representative of Rome. But he was not a miracle worker, and he knew it. His life was in balance. He knew who he was. He knew his limitations. And knew where to go for help.

Jesus agreed to go with the men to the centurion's house, but before they reached the house, the centurion sent a message to Jesus. Here's the message,

> "Lord, do not trouble yourself, for I am not worthy to have you come under my roof. Therefore I did not presume to come to you. But say the word, and let my servant be healed. For I too am a man set under authority, with soldiers under me: and I say to one, 'Go,' and he goes; and to another, 'Come,' and he comes; and to my servant, 'Do this,' and he does it."[14]

Notice his humility, "I am not worthy." This warrior knew himself. He didn't believe the accolades of the town's people about how great a man he was. He knew better. He was a warrior. He had skills. But ultimately, he was a man not worthy to be in the presence of Jesus, yet had faith in him. Here's Jesus' response to the centurion's message, "When Jesus heard these things, he marveled at him, and turning to the crowd that followed him, said, 'I tell you, not even in Israel have I found such faith.'"[15]

In the wisdom of the fictional Detective Harry Callaghan, "A good man always knows his limitations." Warriors have a part in making things right, but they can't take on the responsibly to right every wrong, stop every hurt, and save every victim. The centurion knew his limitations and called out in faith to Jesus.

Another issue troubling to officers that I've noticed lately is labeling. This is Psychology 101. When I was a supervisor in the Sex Crimes Unit, if I heard it once, I heard it a thousand times, about a young victim of a sexual assault, "She'll never be the same" or "He's ruined for life." That's simply not true for the vast majority of sex crime victims, even the youngest. Will the experience change their life? Most likely. Will they remember it for the rest of their lives? Probably so. But don't project a ruined life on them by sticking on a label. People, especially children, are resilient and come back stronger with proper counseling and time. Unfortunately, I'm seeing LEOs themselves fall for the trap of labeling.

Policing is a tough career. Law enforcement officers are called do things, see things, and handle things that are horrible and tragic. And there are plenty of loudmouths who disparage officers every chance they get. But I'm not referring to those who hate LEOs. I'm referring to those who support our warriors. Well-meaning people who unintentionally project unhealthy labels on them. Labels such as burned-out, stressed-out, and even mental disorders. Will the experiences on the job change their life? Most likely. Will they remember them for the rest of their lives? Probably so. But don't project a ruined life on them by sticking on a label! In counseling officers, I've noticed officers are self-diagnosing with unhealthy stress, various mental disorders, and even post-traumatic stress. Sadly, some officers use the job to excuse harmful or inappropriate behavior. Sometimes the behavior is self-destructive and sometimes hurts others. Either way, it's not acceptable.

Should officers seek counsel? Absolutely! The wise King Solomon recommended counsel, "Where there is no guidance, a people falls, but in an abundance of counselors there is safety."[16] If my truck isn't running right, I take it to an automotive professional. If my body aches, I go to a medical professional. If my mind is not right, I seek counsel from a mental health professional. If my spirit isn't right, I seek guidance from a spiritual health professional—they are typically called clergy. But be wary of the shade-tree mechanic, the quack doctor, the self-ordained counselor, or the religious phony.

$\backsim$

The triad of tragedy—pain, guilt, and death—is trumped by the *triad of joy*: faith, hope, and love. The Apostle Paul wrote, "So now faith, hope, and love abide, these three; but the greatest of these is love."[17] But we just simply can't decide to have hope. Frankl agrees,

> [O]ptimism is not anything to be commanded or ordered. One cannot even force oneself to be optimistic indiscriminately, against all odds, against all hope. What is true for hope is also true for the other two components of the triad inasmuch as faith and love cannot be commanded or ordered either.[18]

Hope naturally ensues from love through faith.

Hope is why we live. But it should not be hope in humanity, or even hope in one's self. But it should be a hope in that which transcends humanity, time, and space. A hope that all will be made right. A hope that the meaning of life surpasses this world and lives on into eternity.

Faith is why we hope. Hope comes through faith. Faith must have an object. The object of our faith needs to be in the one true God. The evidence demonstrates that the God presented in the Bible is true and can be trusted. He has promised to restore things to the way they were, "He will wipe away every tear from their eyes, and death shall be no more, neither shall there be mourning, nor crying, nor pain anymore, for the former things have passed away."[19] The triad of tragedy will be made right: pain will end, guilt will be forgiven, and death will be defeated.

Love is why we have faith. Why is love the greatest? Because faith and hope depend on love. Love encompasses faith and hope. Without love, there's no object for faith and without faith there's no hope. "In this the love of God was made manifest among us, that God sent his only Son into the world, so that we might live through him."[20] Our ultimate hope is faith in God for eternal salvation, "Christ in you, the hope of glory."[21] Although we obtain God's salvation in Christ when we put faith in him, salvation will not be fully realized in our life on earth.

In the meantime, we remain here where pain and suffering continue. Why? Because evil continues. Why does evil continue? It's not because God lacks love, it's because he is love. Love is patient. God is patient. He is patient because he does not want anyone to perish. The Apostle Peter wrote, "The Lord...is patient toward you, not wishing that any should perish, but that all should reach repentance."[22]

~

How can we live in hope in a fallen world? It's not enough to know these things intellectually. We must live them practically. It begins with a transformation in our thinking. It is a renewal of the mind. Renewal of the mind means thinking differently. Scott Achor, in his best seller, *The Happiness Advantage*, writes that success is a by-product of happiness, not the other way around.[23] He says that for years we've been taught that success brings happiness. This is why we are driven to succeed. *Succeed and you will be happy!* However, those of us who've lived long enough, have learned by experience that's just not true. Oh, you'll be happy for a moment, but you'll soon want more. Achor found that happy people are more successful. *Be happy and you will succeed!* Hence, for businesses, he recommends that owners and managers look for ways to keep their employees happy and the result will be a more productive workforce.

However, happiness is based on *happenings*. Something *happens* that makes you happy. It might be a joke someone tells, a present you receive, a compliment someone gives, or a feat you've accomplished. Achor demonstrates a happy worker makes a more productive worker. Yet, the goal is the same—the company's bottom line. So, this seems circular. Not only that, happiness goes just as quickly as it comes. If wealth, position, fame, or power brought lasting satisfaction, there would be no suicides among those who have achieved the things most people dream about.

Happiness doesn't cut it. Success doesn't cut it. What we are really searching for is contentment—a peace that is beyond understanding.

Those who have placed their faith in Christ for salvation have conquered the law of sin and death but remain in the physical body. That means, while still here, we remain subject to the realm of sin and death. We still face pain and suffering. However, we are to think differently. The Apostle Paul wrote, "whatever is true, whatever is honorable, whatever is just, whatever is pure, whatever is lovely, whatever is commendable, if there is any excellence, if there is anything worthy of praise, think about these things."[24] Thinking differently means reasoning differently.

Some try to soothe pain and suffering not by thinking differently, but by quoting Bible verses. One of the most popular in difficult times is, "I can do all things through him [Christ] who strengthens me."[25] But, it is also one of the most misunderstood and misapplied verses in the Bible. The verse is quietly muttered by the athletic trying to push his body to the limit. It's given as an encouragement for one scared to make their first jump off the high dive. It's quoted as encouragement when facing a tough exam. In many ways it's used as some kind of good-luck charm. It's as if one can summon the power of Christ to achieve whatever is challenging them by quoting this verse.

But isn't that what the verse says? "I can do *all things*...." Yes, that is what it says when ripped from its context! When ripped from its context you and I can do *all things* through the power of Christ. How about jumping off a cliff and flying? How about stopping a train with your bare hands? How about flying a commercial plane with no training? How about shooting a sub-70 round of golf your first time out?

"That's ridiculous" you say. "That's not what the Apostle meant." Yes, I agree that is ridiculous, and that's not what he meant. But where do we draw the line? Wouldn't these things be included with *all things*? If these things weren't what Paul was talking about, then what were the things he spoke of? The things he was speaking about were the things mentioned in the preceding verse, "I know how to be brought low, and I know how to abound. In any and every circumstance, I have learned the secret of facing plenty and hunger, abundance and need."[26]

The Apostle is saying that *in Christ* we are able to remain content no matter the circumstance. Another translation better captures the idea by inserting the pronoun "this." "I can do all *this* through him who gives me strength."[27] "This" refers to what precedes.

Contentment comes from right thinking and practical experience. "I have learned in whatever situation I am to be content."[28] Paul learned contentment. It wasn't given. It wasn't discovered. It was learned. The Apostle spoke from experience; he had endured suffering the likes of which few have seen, and, in the end, he was martyred for his faith.

Many times, pain and suffering must be endured. However, we know they will come to an end. Guilt is forgiven. Death is conquered. And therein is hope.

EPILOGUE

Law enforcement officers are a lot of things, sometimes even someone's homework assignment. In the late 1980s, a lady from my church was attending classes at the University of Texas at San Antonio and asked if I could speak to her class to fulfill an assignment. I agreed to do so. When called upon, I went to the front of the class, introduced myself, and talked about policing in San Antonio. I fielded several questions, none of which I remember, but one. To this day I recall a student asking me, "How can you be a Christian and be a police officer?" The first thought that came to my mind was, "I don't know if I could be a police officer without being a Christian!" And that's what I said. This young person's view of LEOs was influenced by the media's negative reporting. The media reporting on the police hasn't changed over the years. From the riots of the 1960s to present, there has always been a negative bias against law enforcement. Some of this is our own fault. We've made mistakes, and we need to own them. I've never opposed reporting the truth, but it irks me that the vast majority of what is reported is negative and too many headlines are written to disparage officers.

The onslaught of negative reporting fuels the "us versus them" mentality and works to divide police-community relationships. Officers shouldn't believe all the negative press and realize the majority of the public supports them. If officers start to believe that everyone is against them, they *will lose their focus of service and protection. The moral compass inside each of us can be corrupted and take us off course if we don't set it to true North and keep our focus.*

Policing is an honorable and rewarding career. However, if we allow it, it can be a dishonorable and unrewarding chore. Like all careers, law enforcement is temporary. Most officers retire after twenty or so years and move on to another career. Some stay with policing for thirty or forty years. But eventually it will end. Officers need to guard against their occupation defining who they are. Policing is what you do, not who you are. Who you are is much more important. While our life's meaning may encompass policing, there's more to life than that. Policing is temporary.

Many LEOs find the transition from officer to civilian tough. Receiving my first badge number was one of the highlights of my life. But, not long into my career, a veteran officer helped me see reality. "Remember, Tim," he said, "to the city, you're nothing more than a number. When you leave, that number will be given to someone else." At the time I thought, "Boy what a cynical perspective." But as I thought about it, the wisdom of his advice was transitional. Early on I understood that life was more than a career. Life has a deeper meaning. My career as a police officer was simply part of a bigger plan for my life. Although honorable, policing is simply the things of man. When we believe that the things of man (be it position, power, or prestige) are what gives life meaning, we will be disappointed. Sometimes profoundly disappointed. And when we are, other options are considered, even suicide.

Although the gloomy statistics of suicide may shock us, the fact is, the vast majority of law enforcement officers and combat veterans don't take their own lives. Suicide can be defeated. It can be overcome. Most warriors live long and productive lives. What keeps them going? Hope. Inside each one of us is that elusive yearning we call hope. A hope for something more, something new, something better. The key is not to let the light of hope go out.

As mentioned in the preceding chapters, LEOs see a lot. They are called upon to do a lot, to do things most people cringe at the thought of doing. As I finish this book, America is racked by riots that were prompted by the in-custody death of George Floyd. Law enforcement officers across the country have stepped up to protect the life and property of people they don't know and some who don't even like them. Some officers have died as a result. Many have been injured. The spouses, children, and parents of these warriors stay home and pray their officer will return home safely.

So, how do we hope while living in a fallen world? A world that can't be trusted. A world that seems to be spinning out of control. A world filled with hatred. A world that betrays us. We do so with the other two gifts that have been given to each of us—faith and love. Hope, faith, and love are gifts God gave to humans. The greatest of these is love.

We must have a hope that goes beyond the temporal pleasures the world offers. If our hope is in these things, we will be disappointed. We have a hope that goes beyond more—that there is a forever. A hope that goes beyond new—that all things will be made new. A hope that goes beyond better—that a perfect world awaits. Hope is a gift and, like all of God's gifts, it must be opened. When we open God's gift of hope we find much more than we imagined.

How do we find this hope? Faith. Faith produces hope. We hope because our faith is not in the things of man, but in God. In a God whose knowledge, power, and love are incomprehensible. We may not understand why he doesn't use his power to end suffering, but we trust his love. Therefore, we hope.

Because we hope we endure. Law enforcement officers and soldiers train and prepare for conflict. Conflict is why there is combat. The true warrior doesn't shirk at conflict, but grasps at it, endures it, and is victorious over it. Warriors not only endure suffering; they embrace it like a foe to be defeated. In fact, warriors welcome suffering because it builds character that produces hope. The Apostle Paul said as much, "We rejoice in our sufferings, knowing that suffering produces endurance, and endurance produces character, and character produces hope."[1] Enduring struggles honorably will produce a character that is tested. A tested character produces "a deeper conviction of the reality and certainty for that which we hope."[2]

What is the reality and certainty that we hope for? Meaning. Viktor Frankl knew and accepted that suffering is part of living, but he also understood that suffering can be endured when it has purpose. Frankl writes, "In some way, suffering ceases to be suffering at the moment it finds meaning."[3] Where does man's search for meaning end? It ends at God's love. "God *shows his love for us in that while we were still sinners, Christ died for us."*[4] *Why is God's love so important? Because God's love offers forgiveness.*

Forgiven. What a powerful word. True forgiveness is always accompanied by mercy and love. King David penned the Warrior's Prayer: "Have mercy on me, O God, according to your steadfast love; according to your abundant mercy blot out my transgressions. Wash me thoroughly from my iniquity, and cleanse me from my sin!"[5] *We are only forgiven by God through the death of Jesus, "In him we have redemption through his blood, the forgiveness of our trespasses, according to the riches of his grace."*[6]

The triad of tragedy (pain, guilt, and death) is answered by the triad of joy (hope, faith, and love). Pain will end, guilt will be forgiven, and will be death defeated.

The centurion of Luke chapter 7 knew his limitations and called out to Jesus in faith. Will you do the same? Right now, where you are, you can put your faith in Jesus alone for salvation. Receive God's gift of salvation that is only offered by his grace, apart from any works.

∼

M an's search for meaning ends with God's love. *"For God so loved the world, that he gave his only Son, that whoever believes in him should not perish but have eternal life."*[7]

∼

T hanks for reading. If you are interested in a group study based on *Suicide is Not an Option,* please go to:

TheStrongBlueLine.org/resources

From there you can download free discussion question sheets for each chapter.

WORKS CITED

Achor, S. (2010). *The Happiness Advantage: The Seven Principles of Positive Psychology that Fuel Success and Performance at Work*. New York: Crown Publishing Company.

Barna Research Group. (2015, March 24). *2015 State of Atheism in America*. Retrieved May 2020, from Barna.com: https://www.barna.com/research/2015-state-of-atheism-in-america/

Barr, W. (2019, December 16). *Barr: Rising disrespect for cops not only wrong, it puts us in danger*. Retrieved May 2020, from New York Post: https://nypost.com/2019/12/16/barr-rising-disrespect-for-cops-not-only-wrong-it-puts-us-in-danger/

Below 100. (2019). *About*. Retrieved from Below 100: https://www.below100.org/vision-mission/

Blomberg, C. L. (1992). *The New American Commentary, Matthew*. Nashville: Broadmand Press.

Blue HELP. (2020). *Officer Suicide Statistics*. Retrieved April 2020, from Blue HELP: https://bluehelp.org/resources/statistics/

Bourke, R., Rocco, T., & Black, C. (1983). A Little Good News. *A Little Good News*.

Carson, D. (1991). *Pillar New Testament Commentary, John*. Grand Rapids: Wm. B. Eerdmans Publishing Company.

Corduan, W. (1997). *No Doubt About It.* Nashville: Broadman and Holman.

Dobson, J. (2016). *Voyaging Through Life's Transitions: Guilt the Painful Emotion.* Retrieved from James Dobson's Family Talk: http://www.drjamesdobson.org/articles/voyage/guilt-the-painful-emotion

Dylan, B. (2020). *Bob Dylan, Quotes, Quotable Quote.* Retrieved May 2020, from Goodreads.com: https://www.goodreads.com/quotes/7966189-if-you-re-not-busy-being-born-you-re-busy-dying

Eby, A. (2018). *Northeastern University College of Social Sciences and Humanities.* Retrieved April 2020, from What Would Plato Do?: https://cssh.northeastern.edu/ethics/what-would-plato-do-alexandra-eby/

Edwards, J. R. (2015). *The Piller New Testament Commentary, The Gospel According to Luke.* Nottingham: Wm. B. Eerdamans Publishing Co.

Evans, D. (2020, April 16). San Antonio Police Sergeant. (T. Rupp, Interviewer)

Federal Bureau of Investigation. (2019). *2018 Law Enforcement Officers.* Retrieved April 2020, from FBI: UCR: https://ucr.fbi.gov/leo-ka/2018/topic-pages/officers-assaulted

Ferry, L. (2011). *A Brief History of Thought.* New York: Harper Collins.

Frankl, V. (2006). *Man's Search for Meaning.* Boston: Beacon Press.

Gallup. (2016). *More than 9 in 10 Americans Continue to Believe in God.* Retrieved from gallup.com: http://www.gallup.com/home.aspx?g_source=logo

Grossman, D. (1995). The Bullet Proof Mind audio seminar.

Grudem, W. (1994). *Systematic Theology.* Grand Rapids: Zondervan.

Grudem, W. (1999). *Bible Doctrines.* Grand Rapids: Zondervan.

Harent, S. (2017). *Original Sin.* (K. Knight, Producer, & New Advent) Retrieved April 2020, from Catholic Encyclopedia: http://www.newadvent.org/cathen/11312a.htm

Hilliard, J. (2019, September 14). *New Study Shows Police at Highest*

Risk for Suicide of any Profession. Retrieved June 2020, from Addiction Center: https://www.addictioncenter.com/news/2019/09/police-at-highest-risk-for-suicide-than-any-profession/

Hunter, D. (2020, January 14). *Police officer suicide rate more than doubles line-of-duty deaths in 2019, study shows*. Retrieved from Fox News: https://www.foxnews.com/us/texas-police-officer-suicide-rate?utm_source=feedburner&utm_medium=feed&utm_campaign=Feed%3A%20 foxnews%2Fnational%20%28Internal%20-%20US%20Latest%20-%20Text%29

Huxley, A. (2020). *Aldous Huxely Quotes*. Retrieved July 2020, from goodreads.com: https://www.goodreads.com/quotes/465563-i-had-motives-for-not-wanting-the-world-to-have

Jennings, W. (1984). Gemini Song [Recorded by W. Jennings]. On *Never Could Toe the Mark*. Nashville, Tennesee, USA: W. Jennings, D. Cartee, A. Cartee, & B. Cartee.

Lewis, C. (1941, November 1). The Weight of Glory. *Theology, 43*, pp. 263-274.

Mayo Clinic Staff. (2020). *Sudden Infant Death Syndrome*. Retrieved April 2020, from Mayo Clinic: https://www.mayoclinic.org/diseases-conditions/sudden-infant-death-syndrome/symptoms-causes/syc-20352800

McCallum, D. (2019). *Essays, Five Worldviews*. Retrieved April 2020, from Xenos Christian Fellowship: https://www.xenos.org/essays/five-worldviews

McCormick, M. (n.d.). *Immanuel Kant: Metaphysics*. Retrieved April 2020, from Internet Encyclopedia of Philosophy: https://www.iep.utm.edu/kantmeta/#SH8a

Merriam-Webster. (2020). *Offense*. Retrieved April 2020, from Merriam-Webster: https://www.merriam-webster.com/dictionary/offense

Merriam-Webster. (2020, April 12). *Science*. Retrieved April 2020, from Merriam-Webster Dictionary: https://www.merriam-webster.com/dictionary/science

Merriam-Webster. (2020, April 16). *Society*. Retrieved April 2020, from Merrian-Webster Dictionary: https://www.merriam-webster.com/dictionary/society

Moo, D. J. (1996). *The Espistle to the Romans.* Grand Rapids: William B. Eerdmans Publishing Company.

Moore, D. (2020, April 7). Police Officer, Retired. (T. Rupp, Interviewer)

Morris, L. (1988). *Tyndale New Testament Commentaries, Luke.* Downers Grove: InterVarsity Press.

National Academy of Sciences. (2002). *Reducing Suicide: A National Imperative.* Retrieved from National Center for Biotechnology Information: https://www.ncbi.nlm.nih.gov/books/NBK220933/

National Institute of Mental Health. (2019, April). *Mental Health Information.* Retrieved from National Institute of Mental Health: https://www.nimh.nih.gov/health/statistics/suicide.shtml

Nelson's New Illustrated Bible Dictionary. (1995). *Nelson's New Illustrated Bible Dictionary.* (R. F. Youngblood, Ed.) Nashville, TN, USA: Thomas Nelson Pulishers.

Packer, J. (2015, October 21). *Crossway.* Retrieved May 2020, from Where There's Hope, There's Life: https://www.crossway.org/articles/where-theres-hope-theres-life/

Panayi, A. (2020, Apirl 3). *COVID-19 Is Likely to Lead to an Increase in Suicides.* Retrieved April 2020, from Scientific American: https://blogs.scientificamerican.com/observations/covid-19-is-likely-to-lead-to-an-increase-in-suicides/

Rand, D. G., Green, J. D., & Nowak, M. A. (2012, September 20). *Spontaneous giving and calculated greed.* Retrieved April 2020, from Nature.com: https://www.nature.com/articles/nature11467.epdf? referrer_access_token=
sP7CWZRCqRd4vh1yCO9WDNRgNojAjWel9jnR3ZoTv0OuWnzgZ WIYIT6G8DCrDRW76b7kYf3RDJyFwM1lGJ_CWxJEPz0SXdPQuFml yicm GYBjF3mWoenarhSFLiLXRHnzHWFKtpYuAHPMtkzPyUyx-VkQ8ZFqKuTUi_vg4LK-5VlY3hqJB61Q4je

Rupp, T. (1995, January 6). Capital Murder SAPD Case 95-010785. *Supplemental Report.* San Antonio, Texas, United States of America.

Rupp, T. (2016). *Winning a Gunfight.* Idaho Falls: The Strong Blue Line.

Rupp, T. (2018). *Winning is More than Surviving.* Idaho Falls: The Strong Blue Line.

Ryrie, C. C. (2020). *Charles C. Ryrie Quotes*. Retrieved June 2020, from Good Reads: https://www.goodreads.com/author/quotes/142712. Charles_C_Ryrie

Shannon, K. (1995, October 24). *AP News*. Retrieved April 2020, from Prosecutors: 13-year-old-Murder Suspect Loved Horrors: https://apnews.com/0c22e8e147f927eb1ca83044588b955a

Tucker, A. (2013, January). *Are Babies Born Good?* Retrieved April 2020, from Smithsonian Magazine: https://www.smithsonianmag.com/science-nature/are-babies-born-good-165443013/

United Religions Initiative. (2020). *Hinduism: Basic Beliefs*. Retrieved April 2020, from United Religions Initiative: https://uri.org/kids/world-religions/hindu-beliefs

United Religions Initiative. (2020). *Islam: Basic Beliefs*. Retrieved April 2020, from United Religions Initiative: https://uri.org/kids/world-religions/muslim-beliefs

University of Idaho. (n.d.). *Jean-Jacques Rousseau*. Retrieved April 2020, from University of Idaho webpages: https://www.webpages.uidaho.edu/engl_258/Lecture%20Notes/man_is_naturally_good.htm

Vine, W. U. (1984). *Vine's Complete Expository Dictionary of Old and New Testament Words*. Nashville: Thomas Nelson Publishers.

Wallace, J. W. (2015). *God's Crime Scene*. Colorado Springs: David C. Cook.

Walsh, A., & Hemmens, C. (2016). *Law, Justice, and Society*. New York: Oxford University Press, Inc.

Whitbourne, S. K. (2012, August 11). *The Definitive Guide to Guilt*. Retrieved from Psychology Today: https://www.psychologytoday.com/blog/fulfillment-any-age/201208/the-definitive-guide-guilt

Wiersbe, W. (1979). *Be Ready*. Wheaton: Victor Books.

ABOUT THE AUTHOR

Tim Rupp was a career police officer before being called into fulltime vocational ministry. He enlisted in the Air Force after graduating high school. After his enlistment, Tim joined the San Antonio Police Department (SAPD) and gave 24 years of dedicated service before retiring in 2007. During his SAPD career he worked as a patrol officer, homicide detective, patrol sergeant, sex crimes sergeant, police academy supervisor, and internal affairs sergeant-investigator. He continued his law enforcement service as a reserve deputy with the Bonneville County Sheriff's Office, Idaho from 2009-2020.

Before retiring from the SAPD, Tim was called to pastor Elm Creek Baptist Church in La Vernia, TX, just outside of San Antonio. Following his retirement in 2007, he was called to pastor fulltime in

Idaho Falls, where he pastored until 2020. In 2016, Tim founded The Strong Blue Line Ministries to reach law enforcement officers. In 2017, he and a group of active and retired police officers planted Cop Church Idaho Falls. In 2020, Tim retired from being a fulltime pastor to cofound the Law Enforcement Chaplaincy of Idaho. He is committed to serving LEOs and their families fulltime. Tim is available to teach seminars for police officers, churches, and men's groups. For more information or to contact Tim, go to TheStrongBlue-Line.org.

Tim is an ordained minister with the Christian and Missionary Alliance and serves as a Law Enforcement Chaplain in SE Idaho. He graduated from Texas State University (Master of Science in Criminal Justice), Southwestern Baptist Theological Seminary (Master of Divinity and Master of Arts in Christian Education), and Western Seminary (Doctor of Ministry). He is married to Sherry and they have three children, Christina, Aaron, and Emily and several grandchildren.

OTHER TITLES BY TIM RUPP

Available on Amazon or discounted in bulk order at The Strong Blue Line (TheStrongBlueLine.org).

Non-Fiction:

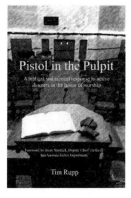

Pistol in the Pulpit, A biblical and tactical response to active shootings in the house of worship, 2016.

Active Shooter—a term recently coined that sends chills up the spines of principles, teachers, parents...and now pastors and parishioners. The FBI defines an active shooter as "an individual actively engaged in killing or attempting to kill people in a confined and populated area, typically through the use of firearms." Active Killer is a more fitting term. What is the biblical approach to this threat? Christians are struggling with how to respond. Do we trust God and pray for his protection? Do we "turn the other cheek" and do nothing when someone threatens to kill us? Do we take up arms to defend ourselves and others? Christians who choose the responsibility of employing lethal force must be informed by both a spiritual and tactical foundation. Not only is there a proper biblical response, there is also a proper tactical response. What are these proper responses? These critical questions are answered in *Pistol in the Pulpit*.

Winning a Gunfight, Securing victory ethically, mentally, and tactically in a gunfight, 2016.

Does physically surviving a gunfight mean you won? Not by a long shot. Many people survive gunfights. In fact, most people who are in a gunfight survive. But there's a difference between surviving and winning. Surviving means you continue to exist. Continuing to exist and winning are not the same. Career police officer and author Tim Rupp has been on both sides of a gunfight—being investigated after being in a gunfight and investigating citizens and officers who have been in shootings. Drawing from personal and professional experiences as a patrol officer, homicide detective, and police sergeant, Rupp takes you through what you'll face in a gunfight. Before picking up a gun for personal protection or the protection of others you need to prepare yourself for what you'll face before, during, and after a gunfight. *Winning a Gunfight* prepares you ethically, mentally, and tactically how to win a gunfight. *Winning a Gunfight* is a must read for police officers, military, and armed citizens.

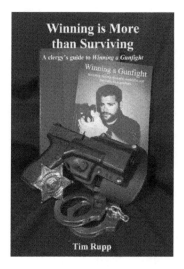

Winning is More than Surviving, A clergy's guide to *Winning a Gunfight, 2018.*

Police and military chaplains are called on to minister to those who kill.

Violence is shunned in our society, but justified violence is sometimes necessary to stop unjustified violence. Even the wise King Solomon said, there is "a time to kill" (Eccl. 3:3). While most of society recoils in fear at violence, some are called to enter that violent world and protect.

There are warriors among us who take up arms and protect those unable or unwilling to protect themselves. But who helps the warriors? Chaplains are called to minister to the spiritual needs of these warriors. To be effective, members of the clergy need to understand the dynamics of using lethal force. *Winning is More than Surviving* is a supplemental guide to *Winning a Gunfight* for clergy to use as they minister to these warriors.

There are warriors among us who take up arms and protect those unable or unwilling to protect themselves. But who helps the warriors? Chaplains are called to minister to the spiritual needs of these warriors. To be effective, members of the clergy need to understand the dynamics of using lethal force. *Winning is More than Surviving* is a supplemental guide to *Winning a Gunfight* for clergy to use as they minister to these warriors.

Fiction

Vengeance Is Mine, The Luke Horn Saga Begins, 2017.

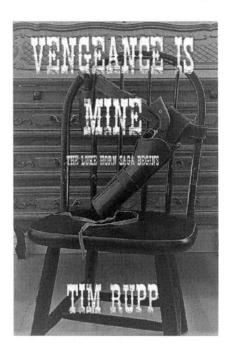

It was 1863, America was split by war. Texas farmer and former lawman, Levi Horn is called to serve for the South, leaving his teenage son to watch over the family. A band of outlaws led by a revenge-driven escaped convict attacks Horn's family and farm. Torn between vengeance and justice, sixteen-year-old Luke Horn sets off on the trail of the outlaws.

Vengeance Is Mine Too, The Luke Horn Saga Continues, 2019.

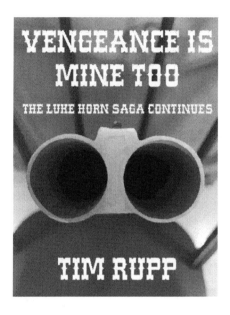

Just when you think the adventure is over, you find it just began. Luke, Joe Ray, and Jack aren't finished righting wrongs. The Civil War was tearing America apart and renegade Confederate soldiers were wreaking havoc in Texas. The outlaw soldiers made the mistake of thinking Luke was still a boy. He wasn't. Luke was forced into manhood and accepted the responsibilities manhood demands while he struggled with his own demons.

Warriors For the Faith, First-person stories from the Bible, 2018.

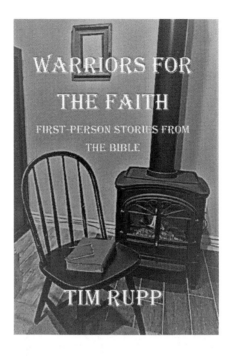

Life is a story. A good movie or book places us "in" the action. We feel like we can relate to, and understand the characters. We cheer for the hero and disdain the villain. Two-thirds of the Bible is written in historical narrative —stories about people. Jesus taught using stories. The stories in the Bible are replete with drama, mystery, and even humor. Like popular movies and novels, Bible stories have intriguing plots of love, friendship, betrayal, competition, murder, and war. Yet, many times they seem boring and we have trouble relating to the characters. Through first-person historical narrative, Pastor Tim Rupp brings biblical characters to life and allows them to tell their stories.

NOTES

Preface

1. (Barr, 2019)

1. Paradise Lost

1. (Hilliard, 2019)
2. (National Academy of Sciences, 2002)
3. (National Institute of Mental Health, 2019)
4. (Frankl, 2006, p. 90)
5. (1 Thessalonians 5:23, emphasis added.)
6. (Hebrews 4:12, emphasis added.)
7. (Rupp, Winning a Gunfight, 2016, p. 9)
8. (Frankl, 2006, p. 116)

2. The Light of Hope

1. (Packer, 2015)
2. (Name has been changed.)
3. (Federal Bureau of Investigation, 2019)
4. (Rupp, Winning is More than Surviving, 2018)
5. (Below 100, 2019)
6. (Blue HELP, 2020)
7. (Hunter, 2020)

3. Hope is Why we Live

1. (1 Corinthians 13:13)
2. (Judges 9:54)
3. (1 Samuel 31:4)
4. (Judges 16:28-30)
5. (1 Samuel 31:5, emphasis added.)
6. (2 Samuel 17:23, emphasis added.)
7. (1 Kings 16:18, emphasis added.)
8. (Luke 6:12-16)
9. (Morris, 1988, p. 321)
10. (Nelson's New Illustrated Bible Dictionary, 1995, pp. 713-714)

11. (Mark 8:31-32a)
12. (Mark 8:32b-33)
13. (Mark 10:35-36)
14. (Mark 9:31-32, emphasis added.)
15. (Carson, 1991, p. 429)
16. (John 12:6)
17. (Matthew 6:21)
18. (Mark 8:33b)
19. (John 18:36)
20. (Luke 22:3-4)
21. (Ephesians 2:1-3a, emphasis added.)
22. (Luke 22:5-6)
23. (Edwards, 2015, p. 618)
24. (Blomberg, 1992, p. 386)
25. (Matthew 27:3)
26. (Matthew 27:4-5)

4. Hope Gives Life Meaning

1. (Panayi, 2020)
2. (Frankl, 2006, p. 18)
3. (Frankl, 2006, p. 107)
4. (Frankl, 2006, p. 105)
5. (Huxley, 2020)
6. (Frankl, 2006, p. 138)
7. (Frankl, 2006, pp. 137-138)
8. (Lewis, 1941)
9. (Ecclesiastes 3:11)
10. (Bourke, Rocco, & Black, 1983)
11. (Revelation 22:5)
12. (Revelation 21:5)
13. (Hebrews 10:14)
14. (Lewis, 1941)
15. (Lewis, 1941)
16. (Lewis, 1941)
17. (Lewis, 1941)

5. Faith in People

1. ("REDRUM" was from a horror movie named *The Shinning*.)
2. (Genesis 6:5)
3. (Ecclesiastes 7:20)
4. (Grudem, Systematic Theology, 1994, p. 490)
5. (Eby, 2018)
6. (Walsh & Hemmens, 2016, p. 12)

7. (Harent, 2017)
8. (Romans 5:12)
9. (Harent, 2017)
10. (Romans 3:22-23)
11. (Romans 2:6)
12. (Colossians 2:25)
13. (Walsh & Hemmens, 2016)
14. (McCormick, n.d.)
15. (Rand, Green, & Nowak, 2012)
16. (University of Idaho, n.d.)
17. (Tucker, 2013)
18. (Jennings, 1984)
19. (Ryrie, 2020)
20. (Gallup, 2016)

6. Faith in Societies, Systems, and Science

1. (Rupp, Capital Murder SAPD Case 95-010785, 1995)
2. (Shannon, 1995)
3. (McCallum, 2019)
4. (McCallum, 2019)
5. (Merriam-Webster, 2020)
6. (Evans, 2020)
7. (Merriam-Webster, 2020)

7. Faith in God

1. (Retired cold-case homicide detective J. Warner Wallace wrote two books that heavily influenced this chapter, *Cold-Case Christianity* and *God's Crime Scene*. I highly recommend these books for a greater and more detailed apologetic on the God of the Bible and Christianity.)
2. (John 4:24)
3. (Genesis 1:1)
4. (Corduan, 1997, p. 53)
5. (Grudem, Systematic Theology, 1994, p. 141)
6. Ritter, Michael E. The Physical Environment: an Introduction to Physical Geography. July 13, 2017. (earthonlinemedia.com/ebooks/tpe_3e/title_page.htm).
7. (Wallace, 2015, pp. 58-60)
8. (Psalm 8:2)
9. https://www.space.com/25126-big-bang-theory.html
10. (Psalm 33:6)
11. (Wallace, 2015, p. 24)
12. (Wallace, 2015, p. 24)
13. (Stott as quoted by Osborne, 2004, p. 48)
14. (Acts 24:16)

15. (Hebrews 11:3)

8. Pain and Love

1. (Mayo Clinic Staff, 2020)
2. (Moore, 2020)
3. (United Religions Initiative, 2020)
4. (United Religions Initiative, 2020)
5. (1 John 4:8,16)
6. (Grudem, Bible Doctrines, 1999, p. 99)
7. (Job 37:5)
8. (1 Corinthians 2:11)
9. (Psalm 145:9)
10. (Isaiah 45:7)
11. (Vine, 1984, p. 51)
12. (Luke 2:14, emphasis added)
13. (Barna Research Group, 2015)
14. (Revelation 21:3-4)
15. (Revelation 21:6, Emphasis added.)
16. (2 Peter 3:9)
17. (Frankl, 2006, p. 138)
18. (Romans 5:3)
19. (Romans 8:18)

9. Guilt and Love

1. (Name has been changed.)
2. (Nelson's New Illustrated Bible Dictionary, 1995, p. 526)
3. (Whitbourne, 2012)
4. (Dobson, 2016)
5. (Merriam-Webster, 2020; Merriam-Webster, 2020)
6. (Whitbourne, 2012)
7. (Romans 2:15)
8. (Colossians 3:13, emphasis added.)
9. (Matthew 6:12)
10. (Psalm 118:8)
11. (Mark 2:5)
12. (Mark 2:6-7)
13. (Romans 6:23)
14. (Matthew 26:28)

10. Death and Love

1. (Ferry, 2011, p. 4)
2. (Hebrews 9:27)
3. (Dylan, 2020)
4. (Genesis 3:1)
5. (Genesis 3:4-5)
6. (Genesis 2:25)
7. (Genesis 3:7)
8. (Genesis 3:19)
9. (Genesis 3:22)
10. (James 1:14-15)
11. (Romans 6:23)
12. (Wiersbe, 1979, p. 83)
13. (1 Thessalonians 4:13)
14. (Genesis 35:18)
15. (2 Corinthians 5:21)
16. (John 3:16)
17. (Mark 10:45)
18. (Romans 5:8)
19. (Romans 8:2)
20. (Romans 6:23)
21. (1 Thessalonians 4:13)

11. Paradise Restored

1. (Revelation 22:5)
2. (Revelation 21:5)
3. (Acts 13:22)
4. (Grossman, 1995)
5. (Information gathered from various media sources.)
6. (Merriam-Webster, 2020)
7. (Deuteronomy 31:7)
8. (Proverbs 28:1)
9. (Romans 13:4)
10. (Matthew 6:12)
11. (Psalm 51:3)
12. (Psalm 51:1-2)
13. (Luke 7:4-5)
14. (Luke 7:6-8)
15. (Luke 7:9)
16. (Proverbs 11:14)
17. (1 Corinthians 13:13)
18. (Frankl, 2006, p. 138)
19. (Revelation 21:4)

20. (1 John 4:9)
21. (Colossians 1:27)
22. (2 Peter 3:9)
23. (Achor, 2010)
24. (Philippians 4:8)
25. (Philippians 4:13)
26. (Philippians 4:12)
27. (Philippians 4:13, NIV, emphasis added.)
28. (Philippians 4:11)

Epilogue

1. (Romans 5:3-4)
2. (Moo, 1996, p. 304)
3. (Frankl, 2006, p. 113)
4. (Romans 5:8)
5. (Psalm 51:1-2)
6. (Ephesians 1:7)
7. (John 3:16)

Made in the USA
Columbia, SC
28 July 2022

64191970R00089